GCSE Religious Studies

CHRISTIAN PERSPECTIVES

Libby Ahluwalia

Hodder Murray

A MEMBER OF THE HODDER HEADLINE GROUP

ACKNOWLEDGEMENTS

The author and publishers thank the following for permission to reproduce copyright photographs in this book:
Ian Smeeton pp 2, 4, 5, 97; Bildarchiv Preussischer Kulturbesitz p 8; 'The Baptism of Christ' by Piero della Francesca, © The National Gallery, London p 9 ; Jenny Matthews/Format p12; Stephanie Maze/Corbis p 13; Nicola Sutton/Life File p 13; Angela Maynard/Life File p 14; 'The Fall from Grace' by Lucas Cranach the elder, Schlesw.-Holst Landesmuseum, AKG London, p 15; RW Jones/Corbis p 17; Fotografia, Inc/Corbis p 19, Melanie Friend/Format p 20; Mother's Union p 25; Mary Evans Picture Library p 28; 'The creation of Adam' by Michelangelo Buonarroti, Sistine Chapel, AKG London p 30; Penny Tweedie/Corbis p 31; Nicola Sutton/Life File p 32; Aubrey J. Slaughter/Life File p 33; Nicola Sutton/Life File p 35; Ulrike Preuss/Format p 37; Neil Bromhall/Science Photo Library p 39; PA Photos/EPA p 42; The Samaritans p 45; St Christopher's Hospice p 49; Macmillan Cancer Relief p 50; Ulrike Preuss/Format p 53; Amel Emric Stringer/Associated Press p 54; Mary Evans Picture Library p 55; Popperfoto p 56; 57; AP/Andre Camara/STR p58; Hulton Deutsch p 59top; Associated Press p 59btm;Popperfoto p 60; Associated Press pp iii & 61; Brenda Prince/Format p 65; Jacky Chapman/Format p 66; Brenda Prince/Format p 67; Emma Lee/Life File p 68; Emmanuel Ortiz/Corbis p 72; Bibliotheque Nationale p 75; Imperial War Museum p 76; National Archives p 77; Jeff Widener/Associated Press p 79; Leif Skoogfors/Corbis p 81; Amnesty International p 82, 83; NASA p 86; Nancy Sefton/Science Photo Library p 88; Jerry Schad/Science Photo Library p 88; 'The Gleaners' by J.F. Millet, Musee d'Orsay, Erich Lessing/AKG London p 89; Mark Edwards/Still Pictures p 90; Tim Davis/Science Photo Library p 91; John Heseltine/Corbis p 92;Barry Mayes/Life File p 94; Associated Press p98; Pavel Rahman Stringer/Associated Press p 99; Jim Loring/Tearfund p 101; Fairtrade p 102; Robert van der Hilst/Corbis p 103; Christian Aid p 104; Cafod p104; The Salvation Army p 105; Stefan Rousseau/PA p 108; Peter Turnley/Corbis p 110; Rajendra Shaw/Traidcraft p 111; Christian Aid p 112; Christian Aid/Nick Davies p 112; Liba Taylor/Action Aid p 113; Cafod p 114; Jon Spaull/Cafod p 115; Geoff Crawford/Tearfund p 116; Adam Woolfitt/Corbis p 121; 'Christ on the cross' by Peter Paul Rubens, Copenhagen, Statens Museum for Art, Erich Lessing/ AKG London p 122; copyright © BBC p 123; ©SAF and Christmas Films MCMXCIX all rights reserved. Courtesy of Icon Film Distribution Ltd. p 125.

Every effort has been made to contact the holders of copyright material but if any have been inadvertently overlooked, the publishers will be pleased to make the necessary alterations at the first opportunity.

Orders: please contact Bookpoint Ltd, 130 Milton Park, Abingdon, Oxon OX14 4SB.
Telephone: (44) 01235 827720, Fax: (44) 01235 400454.
Lines are open from 9.00–6.00, Monday to Saturday, with 24 hour message answering service.

You can also order through our website www.hoddereducation.co.uk

British Library Cataloguing in Publication Data
A catalogue record for this title is available from The British Library

ISBN-10: 0 340 78965 4
ISBN-13: 978 0 340 78965 0

First published 2001
Impression number   10 9 8 7
Year   2007 2006 2005

Copyright © 2001 Libby Ahluwalia

Cover photo by Stephanie Maze / Corbis
Typeset by Wyvern 21, 277 Bath Road, Bristol BS4 3EH
Printed in Italy for Hodder Murray, an imprint of Hodder Education, a member of the Hodder Headline Group, 338 Euston Road, London NW1 3BH

CONTENTS

BACKGROUND

INTRODUCTION

There are many situations where it is important to do the right thing, whether or not you are a Christian. Sometimes, almost everyone agrees about what is right and wrong; for example, nearly everyone would agree that it is wrong to torture animals for fun, and that it is wrong to drink too much and then drive a car. However, there are also a lot of important issues where there is strong disagreement about right and wrong, and when people have very different opinions.

How do Christians decide what is the right way to behave, or the right opinion to have? Often, deciding what is right seems to depend on your own personal feelings; some people might agree with you, and others will disagree, but is there any way of knowing who has the right answer, or even if there is one?

FOR DISCUSSION

Try to make a list of things that you think are always wrong, in everyone's opinion.

For most Christians, the Bible is an important source of information about right and wrong

THE IMPORTANCE OF THE BIBLE

For Christians, the Bible is an important source of information about right and wrong. Christians believe that the Bible is the most important book ever written, and that it comes from God. As well as containing poems, songs, and stories about history, it also gives rules and advice about the right way to live.

In the book of Exodus in the Old Testament there are many different laws which Jews and Christians believe were given to Moses by God. These deal with all sorts of different subjects, for example the correct ways in which to worship, how to treat strangers, and how to behave fairly when borrowing or lending money. The most important of these rules are usually considered to be the Ten Commandments:

Then God spoke all these words:

I am the LORD your God, who brought you out of the land of Egypt, out of the house of slavery; you shall have no other gods before me.

You shall not make for yourself an idol, whether in the form of anything that is in heaven above, or that is on the earth beneath, or that is in the water under the earth. You shall not bow down to them or worship them; for I the LORD your God am a jealous God, punishing children for the iniquity of parents, to the third and the fourth generation of those who reject me, but showing steadfast love to the thousandth generation of those who love me and keep my commandments.

You shall not make wrongful use of the name of the LORD your God, for the LORD will not acquit anyone who misuses his name.

Remember the sabbath day, and keep it holy. Six days you shall labour and do all your work. But the seventh day is a sabbath to the LORD your God; you shall not do any work – you, your son or your daughter, your male or female slave, your livestock, or the alien resident in your towns. For in six days the LORD made heaven and earth, the sea, and all that is in them, but rested the seventh day; therefore the LORD blessed the sabbath day and consecrated it.

Honour your father and your mother, so that your days may be long in the land that the LORD your God is giving you.

You shall not murder.

You shall not commit adultery.

You shall not steal.

You shall not bear false witness against your neighbour.

You shall not covet your neighbour's house; you shall not covet your neighbour's wife, or male or female slave, or ox, or donkey, or anything that belongs to your neighbour. (Exodus 20: 1–17)

Christians believe that these are rules which apply to everyone, in every culture and at every time in history.

The New Testament also gives Christians advice about moral issues. The Gospels tell the story of the life, death and resurrection of Jesus, and contain many examples of Jesus' moral teaching. In Matthew's Gospel, Chapters 5 to 7 are devoted to a collection of Jesus' teaching on moral issues, and this is known as the Sermon on the Mount. Here are some examples:

You have heard that it was said to the people long ago, 'Do not commit murder, and anyone who murders will be subject to judgement.' But I tell you that anyone who is angry with his brother will be subject to judgement.' (Matthew 5: 21–22)

If someone forces you to go one mile, go with him two miles. Give to the one who asks you, and do not turn away from the one who wants to borrow from you. (Matthew 5: 41–42)

No one can serve two masters. Either he will hate the one and love the other, or he will be devoted to the one and despise the other. You cannot serve both God and Money. (Matthew 6: 24)

Christians believe that Jesus was the Son of God, so these teachings are particularly important, because for Christians they are not just one human being's personal opinions, but show how God wants people to behave towards one another.

Some Christians try and make moral decisions by asking themselves what Jesus would have done in a similar situation. If they cannot imagine Jesus telling a little 'white lie', or they know that Jesus would have forgiven the person they feel angry with, then they have a good idea about what to do themselves.

In the New Testament, after the Gospels, are the 'epistles' or letters. These were written by some of the very first Christians, to churches which had only just been started and which were trying to follow Christianity for the first time. The people had no experience of church life, and had not been Christians for very long, so the letters were written to try to explain to them the right ways for Christians to live and to behave towards one another. Christians today still find these letters a valuable source of advice about right and wrong.

For example, the letter to the church in Ephesus warns the people:

But among you there must not be even a hint of sexual immorality, or any kind of impurity, or of greed, because they are improper for God's holy people. Nor should there be obscenity, foolish talk or coarse joking, which are out of place, but rather thanksgiving.

(Ephesians 5: 3–4)

Most Christians believe that the Bible is full of truth, and that reading it is one of the best ways of learning the right answers to moral problems. However, they do not always agree about how the Bible should be understood. Some Christians believe that the Bible was written word for word by God, and that every part of it is equally and perfectly true. Other Christians believe that the Bible was written by people who were inspired by God to use their own understanding and write in their own words, and that some of their writings are more suitable for the time in which they were written than they are for today.

Whichever view Christians hold, the Bible needs to be interpreted when moral decisions have to be made, and Christians have to decide on the best way of applying Biblical teachings to their own situations. Sometimes this can be quite difficult:

- Some moral problems today did not exist when the Bible was written. For example, issues relating to fertility treatment for couples who are having difficulty conceiving children, or to nuclear weapons, or to global warming, are not addressed in the Bible at all, because the Bible was written before these situations were possible. Christians have to use Biblical teachings to try and work out for themselves what the right answers might be – and they do not always agree.

- Sometimes the Bible is not completely consistent about a moral issue. There might be a passage in one part of the Bible which teaches that it can be right to fight in a war, for example, while another passage tells people to love their enemies and to respond to evil with good.

Because the Bible is believed to have great authority, most Christians try to study it on a regular basis. Some set aside a special time during the day, every day, when they can read the Bible quietly on their own and think about how the teaching might be relevant for their lives. Sometimes, they might do this with the help of a handbook, which directs the reader to a different Biblical passage for each day of the year, and provides

Sometimes Christians meet together at each other's houses, to study the Bible together and to give each other support

some explanation of the text and some questions to think about. At other times, Christians might want to read about a particular subject, and they might use the Bible as a kind of reference book and look up the passage that they want. Sometimes, groups of Christians meet in each other's houses, or at school or at their place of work, to study the Bible together and discuss its teaching about different moral issues.

All Christian church services use the Bible as an important part of worship. A passage of the Bible is read to the congregation and, often, the priest or minister will use the passage in his or her sermon. The passage will be explained, and the preacher will try to show the members of the congregation how they might use the teaching of the Bible in their daily lives.

Even though Christians use the Bible regularly and talk about what it means for modern times, they do not always come to the same conclusions. Different Christian Churches sometimes disagree; for example, the Roman Catholic Church and the Methodist Church do not have the same opinions about whether it is right to use contraception. Even within one church congregation in one town, there will probably be a wide range of different opinions about moral issues.

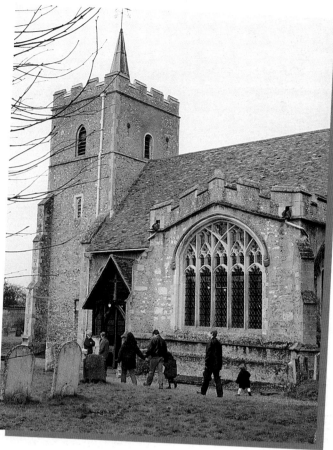

The church plays an important part in the lives of Christians. They can learn about moral issues at Sunday services, but they might not all share the same views

THE ROLE OF THE CHURCH

Most Christians belong to a Church, and do not only worship God when they are on their own but meet regularly with other Christians, at services on Sundays and often at other times as well. The Church can play an important part in helping Christians with moral issues.

- The church is a place where Christians can hear the Bible interpreted and explained. The people who preach in church have usually been to a training college, where they have learned about the history and meanings of the different parts of the Bible, and how to share their knowledge by giving sermons. Although Christians go to church to worship God, they also go to learn.

- The minister or priest will give advice to Christians if they have difficult problems and do not know what to do. Often, there are special times during the week where people can visit the minister or priest and talk privately about something that is worrying them. For example, they

Churches often offer all kinds of activities and support groups for their members and for the community

might have a problem with their marriage, and not know how to solve it. The minister will listen to them, pray for them and help them to find the right way of dealing with the problem. This kind of help is believed to be an important part of the role of the priest or minister.

- In the Roman Catholic tradition, members of the Church can go to confession (the Sacrament of Reconciliation), where with the help of a priest they confess their sins to God. This can help Roman Catholics to deal with moral problems, particularly if they have got themselves into situations which they know to be their own fault. Confession helps them to confront their problems and to make new resolutions about the ways in which they plan to behave in the future.

- Other members of the congregation can also help Christians with moral problems. Many churches have different groups which meet during the week; for example there might be a club for over-60s, a mother-and-toddler group, a men's group and a young people's group. These have regular times where people with similar interests can get together and support each other. Christians might use these groups as a chance to discuss problems and learn from each other's experiences.

- Sometimes, different churches make formal statements about moral issues, such as abortion, euthanasia, war and human rights, explaining what they believe is the right view to hold about moral issues. Members of a church denomination are chosen to meet together, pray, consider the views of the Bible and the traditions of their members, and have long discussions, before eventually coming to an agreement and making a statement. These statements can be useful for individual Christians who want to feel confident that they are making a decision which would be supported by other members of the church to which they belong.

PRAYER

Prayer is a very important part of life for Christians. They believe it is a way in which they can communicate with God, either as part of a group (communal prayer) or quietly on their own (private prayer). Prayer involves speaking to God, and also listening. In the Society of Friends, which is a Christian church often known as the Quakers, the services have a strong emphasis on silence and listening to God, and sometimes the whole of the service can be held in silence. Other churches have services with more varied kinds of worship; but there is always a time for talking and listening to God through prayer. If a Christian has a difficult moral decision to make, one of the first things he or she will probably do is to pray about it, either alone or with Christian friends.

Most Christians would say that God does not answer their questions in an obvious way, with a voice telling them what to do, but that the prayers are answered less directly. Sometimes, they might feel that God gives them a 'sign', to point them in the right direction. For example, if a woman was wondering whether to leave her husband and apply for a divorce, and then, after praying about it, she happened to switch on the television to a programme about the problems divorce can cause for the children in the family, and then she opened the newspaper and saw an article praising marriage counselling, she might believe that this was a sign from God and an answer to her prayers.

Christians believe that direct communication with God through prayer helps them whenever they have a difficult decision to make

CONSCIENCE

Conscience plays an important part in making moral choices, whether or not a person is a Christian. We often feel guilty when we do something wrong, even when we know that no one will find out; and when we think about moral choices, we often know what we ought to do even if we want to do something else. Some Christians believe that the conscience is one of the ways in which God answers prayer and gives guidance. People sometimes cannot explain how they knew which choice to make, but will say 'I just knew it was right.' This feeling can be very strong.

Throughout history, there have been Christians whose consciences have given them strong messages about the right thing to do, and who have refused to go against their consciences even when they were threatened with death. For example, Dietrich Bonhoeffer was a Christian who, during the Second World War, became involved in a

Dietrich Bonhoeffer was a Christian whose conscience led him to become involved in a plan to assassinate Hitler

plot to assassinate Hitler. He knew that he was putting himself in great danger, but his conscience told him that involvement in this plot was the best way of putting his Christian beliefs into action, defending the weak and fighting against evil. Bonhoeffer's plans were discovered and he was executed.

THE HOLY SPIRIT

Christians believe that although there is only one God, he can be understood and experienced in three different ways: this is known as the doctrine of the Trinity. God can be understood as the Father and creator of the world; as the Son, in the person of Jesus; and as the Holy Spirit. They believe that the Holy Spirit lives in every Christian, and can help them, giving them courage when they are afraid, comforting them when they are in trouble, and guiding them when they have decisions to make. Christians believe that if they ask for the guidance of the Holy Spirit before they read the Bible or discuss a problem or make a moral choice, they are more likely to come to the right decision.

The Holy Spirit is very difficult to explain in ordinary language, because it is so different from anything else people experience. Often, it is shown in pictures in the form of a dove. This is because in the story of Jesus' baptism in the Gospels, the Holy Spirit descends on Jesus in a way that is described as being like a dove:

At that time Jesus came from Nazareth in Galilee and was baptised by John in the Jordan. As Jesus was coming up out of the water, he saw heaven and earth being torn open and the Spirit descending on him like a dove.

(Mark1: 9–10)

The dove also symbolises peace, because of the story in Genesis 8 when Noah sent out a dove to see whether the flood was over, and the dove returned with an olive branch in its mouth. Using the symbol of the dove for the Holy Spirit is a way of showing the Christian belief that God can be trusted and everything is going to be all right.

AGAPE

One of the most important things that Christians are supposed to remember when they are making moral decisions is their belief that God is love, and that therefore they should love one another.

When Jesus was asked which of the Old Testament laws he thought was the greatest, he chose two:

In Christian art, the Holy Spirit is often symbolised as a dove

One of the teachers of the law came and heard them debating. Noticing that Jesus had given them a good answer, he asked him, 'Of all the commandments, which is the most important?'

'The most important one,' answered Jesus, 'is this: "Hear, O Israel, the Lord our God, the Lord is one. Love the Lord your God with all your heart and with all your soul and with all your mind and with all your strength." The second is this: "Love your neighbour as yourself." There is no commandment greater than these.'

'Well said, teacher,' the man replied. 'You are right in saying that God is one and there is no other but him. To love him with all your heart, with all your understanding and with all your strength, and to love your neighbour as yourself is more important than all burnt offerings and sacrifices.'

When Jesus saw that he had answered wisely, he said to him, 'You are not far from the kingdom of God.' And from then on no one dared ask him any more questions.

(Mark 12: 28–34)

There are two parts to this teaching: loving God, and loving your neighbour. Loving God means, for Christians, putting God at the centre of their thoughts, and trying to do what God wants. It means spending time with God, listening and taking God's advice, and trying to avoid doing things which hurt God. Loving your neighbour means recognising that everyone else is just as valuable as you are, and treating other people the way that you would like to be treated yourself; this is known as the Golden Rule:

> So in everything, do to others what you would have them do to you, for this sums up the Law and the Prophets.
> (Matthew 7: 12)

When Christians are making moral decisions, they might think about how they would feel if they were the other person, and then try to imagine how they would like to be treated.

The Christian concept of love is known as 'agape', which is a Greek word. The Greeks did not have just one word for love, but several different ones, which showed that love comes in many different forms. For example:

- **Eros** is the name for sexual love, the feelings someone has for a person they find sexually attractive.
- **Philos** is the name for 'brotherly love', the feelings someone might have for a brother or sister, or for a close friend.
- **Storge** is the name for family love and loyalty.

So somebody might feel **eros** for a boyfriend or girlfriend, or even for someone they had never met but seen on the television. They might feel **philos** for their best friend or group of friends, people whose company they enjoy very much; and they might feel **storge** for their cousins, even if they hardly ever see them. Sometimes it is possible to feel more than one kind of love for the same person. In marriages that work really well, all three types of love could be present.

Christians believe that all of these kinds of love come from God, and are good. However, there is another kind of love which is especially important to them, and this is known as **agape**.

Agape is often described as 'unconditional love', which means loving someone else regardless of what they look like, and regardless of how they behave. It has nothing to do with liking them, or whether they like you. It means being concerned about the other person, and wanting the best for them.

The principle of agape is at the centre of all Christian teaching about morality, because for Christians, God does not just approve of love – he actually *is* love:

> Dear friends, let us love one another, for love comes from God. Everyone who loves has been born of God and knows God. Whoever does not love does not know God, because God is love.
>
> This is how God showed his love among us: He sent his one and only Son into the world that we might live through him.
>
> This is love: not that we loved God, but that he loved us and sent his Son as an atoning sacrifice for our sins.
>
> Dear friends, since God so loved us, we also ought to love one another.
>
> No one has ever seen God; but if we love one another, God lives in us and his love is made complete in us. We know that we live in him and he in us, because he has given us of his Spirit. And we have seen and testify that the Father has sent his Son to be the Saviour of the world. If anyone acknowledges that Jesus is the Son of God, God lives in him and he in God. And so we know and rely on the love God has for us. God is love. Whoever lives in love lives in God, and God in him.
>
> In this way, love is made complete among us so that we will have confidence on the day of judgement, because in this world we are like him. There is no fear in love. But perfect love drives out fear, because fear has to do with punishment. The one who fears is not made perfect in love. We love because he first loved us.
>
> If anyone says, 'I love God,' yet hates his brother, he is a liar. For anyone who does not love his brother, whom he has seen, cannot love God, whom he has not seen.
>
> And he has given us this command: Whoever loves God must also love his brother.
> (1 John 4: 7–21)

In this passage, which comes from a letter sent to one of the very new churches in the early days of Christianity, John explains that people should try to live together with love. If they do, they will be sharing God with each other. John shows that, for Christians, the love of God is proved, because God came into the world in Jesus Christ and took away the guilt of human sin.

Perhaps the best-known example of writing about love in the Bible comes from Paul's letter to the Corinthian church. The Christians in Corinth had many arguments with each other, and Paul tried to explain to them what agape love involves. Because the passage is so beautiful and worth remembering, many Christians choose it to be read in church when they get married:

> If I speak in the tongues of men and of angels, but have not love, I am only a resounding gong or a clanging cymbal.
>
> If I have the gift of prophecy and can fathom all mysteries and all knowledge, and if I have a faith that can move mountains, but have not love, I am nothing.
>
> If I give all I possess to the poor and surrender my body to the flames, but have not love, I gain nothing.
>
> Love is patient, love is kind. It does not envy, it does not boast, it is not proud.
>
> It is not rude, it is not self-seeking, it is not easily angered, it keeps no record of wrongs.
>
> Love does not delight in evil but rejoices with the truth.
>
> It always protects, always trusts, always hopes, always perseveres.
>
> Love never fails. But where there are prophecies, they will cease; where there are tongues, they will be stilled; where there is knowledge, it will pass away.
>
> For we know in part and we prophesy in part, but when perfection comes, the imperfect disappears.
>
> When I was a child, I talked like a child, I thought like a child, I reasoned like a child. When I became a man, I put childish ways behind me.

> Now we see but a poor reflection as in a mirror; then we shall see face to face. Now I know in part; then I shall know fully, even as I am fully known.
>
> And now these three remain: faith, hope and love. But the greatest of these is love.
>
> (1 Corinthians 13)

St Augustine of Hippo, who lived from 345 to 440 CE, was one of the greatest thinkers in the history of Christianity. He was concerned that people might think that Christianity was all about following rules and being forbidden from doing things, and he said that Christian morality was much easier than that. He said 'Love, and then do what you will'. He meant that, as long as you act in a loving way, you can do whatever you want. In the 1960s, this was a popular way of understanding Christian morality, and a Christian called Joseph Fletcher wrote a book about it, called *Situation Ethics*, where he explained the same point of view: as long as you look at your situation carefully and put agape into practice, you will be doing the right thing.

However, not everyone agreed with Fletcher. They said that it is not enough to try to put agape into practice, because you might not know what is the most loving way of behaving, and you could make a serious mistake. Christians should use the teaching of the Bible and Church as well.

SUMMARY

Most Christians, therefore, use several different methods at once when they try to make a moral decision:

- They use the teaching in the Bible, which often needs interpretation.
- They take the advice of the Church and of their Christian friends.
- They use their consciences, guided in prayer by the Holy Spirit.
- They try to follow the example of Jesus.
- They try to put the principle of agape into practice.

2

MARRIAGE AND DIVORCE: RELATIONSHIPS WITHIN THE FAMILY

The importance of family life for Christians, and Christian views about the roles of family members. Christian teaching about divorce and annulment, and different Christian opinions about marriage after divorce.

There are many different kinds of families. Some have two parents and their children; in other families, there is one parent, or there might be step-parents, or foster children, or no children, or elderly people might live with their adult sons or daughters. Christians accept that families are all different.

Families are all different. This family has adopted children, and two parents

Most Christians believe that the decisions to marry and to start a family are personal. In some religions, both marriage and parenthood are very much encouraged, but in Christianity it is recognised that some people might choose to remain single. Some of the best-known and most respected Christians have not married, sometimes in order to devote their lives to God in other ways, such as becoming a Catholic priest, a monk or a nun. Jesus himself never married. Some single Christians choose to do important work that does not fit with family life, such as giving medical help to victims of war in dangerous parts of the world. Within Christianity, there has always been a place for single people, who might decide to devote their lives entirely to God instead of getting married.

Some Christians never marry, but devote their lives to God in other ways

Christians believe that family life is important because families provide each other with love, comfort, protection and support. Families have an important role to play in religion:

- Families provide education for the next generation; usually children who are brought up well become responsible adults and will be better parents themselves. Families give children their first experiences of human society and are the best places for children to learn about their rights and responsibilities. They can encourage each other to follow Christianity. If they go to church together and worship together at home, they are all less likely to stop bothering. Parents can also set children a good example of Christian living: they might invite lonely people into their home to share meals, or they might join with the children in a project to raise money for charity. They could show through their own example that they disapprove of gossiping and dishonesty, for example. They can teach the children about Christian festivals and stories, and help them to feel part of the religion.

- The family is the first place where children can find out about love, companionship and forgiveness, in their relationships with their parents and with their brothers and sisters.

Family life is the context in which we learn about love, loyalty and making compromises

- Families have a part to play in the community; they are in the best position to provide hospitality, to give support to other families, to care for the elderly or to adopt unwanted children.

- Most Christians believe that family life is a very important part of a stable society, and that the media should be discouraged from presenting too many negative images of marriage and family relationships (see Chapter. 8).

LIVING TOGETHER

FOR DISCUSSION

Do you think that Christianity should change its views about couples who live together without being married, to keep more up to date?

Marriage is not as popular as it used to be; the number of couples getting married for the first time has been falling steadily since the 1970s. Many people today choose to live together as couples without being married. They might be intending to marry later, if the relationship works, or they might feel that there is no need ever to make the commitment of marriage. Sometimes, people argue that it is impossible to know how you are going to feel about another person in ten or twenty years' time, and so they believe that it is wrong to promise to love someone for ever. They might say that living together helps to prevent taking the other person for granted, because if you treat them badly, then there is no reason for them to stay. Divorce is painful and expensive, but if you are unmarried and living together then you can decide to end the relationship without having to pay a lot of legal fees. It is now quite common for people to have children without being married, and society is much more accepting of this.

However, many Christians believe that there is still an important place for marriage in society. They might say that a relationship cannot develop fully without marriage, because there is always the fear of rejection and the worry that the other person might find someone else more attractive. Quarrels matter more when couples are not married, because there is no commitment to staying together. Christians might say that, if the couple is married, they will remember the promises they have made to each other, and will try much harder to sort out problems rather than just walking away. A Christian might also argue that marriage is the right context for having children, and that God intends children to be born into families where there are two parents who are married to each other.

There are also many Christians who argue that marriage is the only proper context for sex. Roman Catholics believe that the purpose of sex is to join a married couple together and complete their relationship, with the possibility of the birth of children always being present. Sexual relationships outside marriage, such as living together as a couple without being married, are considered by many Christians to be wrong because they interfere with the real purpose of sex as an expression of married love. Most people, however, believe that there is a difference between having sex with someone you are living with, when it is part of a close and loving relationship, and having sex with someone you do not know very well, for example after meeting at a party or on holiday.

Christians believe that there is still an important place for marriage in modern society

BIBLICAL TEACHING ABOUT MARRIAGE

Although there is nothing wrong with choosing to remain single, marriage is seen in the Bible as very valuable, and something that should be taken seriously. In the story of the Creation, in Genesis, God makes Eve as a partner for Adam:

> *So the LORD God caused the man to fall into a deep sleep; and while he was sleeping, he took one of the man's ribs and closed up the place with flesh. Then the LORD God made a woman from the rib he had taken out of the man, and he brought her to the man.*
>
> *The man said, 'This is now bone of my bones and flesh of my flesh; she shall be called "woman", for she was taken out of a man.'*
>
> *For this reason a man will leave his father and mother and be united to his wife, and they will become one flesh.*
>
> (Genesis 2: 21–24)

The book of Genesis teaches that God always intended men and women to be partners for each other

The writers of the Bible show here that they believed God intended, right from the beginning, that men and women should join together for life as couples. The bond between a man and a woman produces new life when children are born, and in this way God's creation continues.

The Bible makes it clear that marriage should be taken very seriously. In particular, it stresses that men and women should be faithful to their wives or husbands. One of the Ten Commandments is:

> *You shall not commit adultery.* (Exodus 20: 14)

Christians believe that it is very important for people who are married to remain faithful to each other, because adultery leads to a lack of trust and shows disrespect for the holiness of marriage. It involves deceit, and it breaks the promises that a husband and wife make to each other when they marry.

However, there is a story which is traditionally placed in John's Gospel, where Jesus surprises a crowd with his attitude towards a woman who has been caught committing adultery:

The teachers of the law and the Pharisees brought in a woman caught in adultery. They made her stand before the group and said to Jesus, 'Teacher, this woman was caught in the act of adultery. In the Law Moses commanded us to stone such women. Now what do you say?'

They were using this question as a trap, in order to have a basis for accusing him. But Jesus bent down and started to write on the ground with his finger.

When they kept on questioning him, he straightened up and said to them, 'If any one of you is without sin, let him be the first to throw a stone at her.'

Again he stooped down and wrote on the ground.

At this, those who heard began to go away one at a time, the older ones first, until only Jesus was left, with the woman still standing there.

Jesus straightened up and asked her, 'Woman, where are they? Has no one condemned you?'

'No one, sir,' she said. 'Then neither do I condemn you,' Jesus declared. 'Go now and leave your life of sin.'

(John 8: 3–11)

FOR DISCUSSION

Do you think that it is reasonable to expect people to stay faithful to one partner for the whole of their lives? Is there really anything wrong with adultery, if the other partner never finds out about it?

Although adultery is regarded as a very serious sin, Christians are encouraged to show compassion and forgiveness, and to think about whether their own behaviour is perfect before they criticise other people.

A CHRISTIAN MARRIAGE

If a couple want to get married in a Christian church, they are often invited to discuss the meaning of Christian marriage with the priest or minister, sometimes in a group with other couples who are also planning their weddings. They will talk about the vows they are going to make, to make sure that they understand what they will be promising to each other. The Church of England teaches that marriage is a gift from God:

Marriage is given, that husband and wife may comfort and help each other, living faithfully together in need and in plenty, in sorrow and in joy. It is given, that with delight and tenderness they may know each other in love, and, through the joy of their bodily union, may strengthen the union of their hearts and lives. It is given as the foundation of family life in which children may be born and nurtured in accordance with God's will, to his praise and glory.

(Common Worship 2000)

In the Roman Catholic tradition, marriage is one of the seven sacraments, which means that it is one of the ways in which people can see a symbol of the bond God creates with people. In marriage, the love between a husband and wife shows something of the love of God.

Christians believe that marriage is very important because within marriage, people learn about love and can express love. They find out the importance of forgiveness, tolerance, comforting each other, celebrating together, appreciating someone else's qualities, and thinking about the well-being of another person. They believe that through marriage, they learn more about God, because God is love (1 John 4).

Through a loving marriage, Christians believe they learn something about the love of God

DIFFERENT ROLES WITHIN THE FAMILY

The Bible teaches that members of a family have responsibilities towards one another.

THE ROLES OF HUSBANDS AND WIVES

There are some Christians who believe that it is the wife's duty to obey her husband, and that her main aim in life should be to support him in his career and to care for any children that they might have. The man should be in charge, and has the responsibility of looking after his wife and children, and providing financial support for the family. They believe that this is what the Bible teaches. They also think that it is important in a relationship for one partner to be the leader, so that when there are disagreements, they can be quickly settled. Men are physically stronger than women, and women are the ones who give birth and breastfeed; therefore, some people say, it is natural for the man to have a leadership role in a family, and for the woman to have the caring, supportive role.

In the New Testament, Paul's letter to the Ephesians explains his views about the ideal relationship between husbands and wives:

Some Christians believe that the role of the husband should be to provide for his family, and the role of the wife should be to support him and look after the children

> *For the husband is the head of the wife as Christ is the head of the church, his body, of which he is the Saviour.*
>
> *Now as the church submits to Christ, so also wives should submit to their husbands in everything.*
>
> *Husbands, love your wives, just as Christ loved the church and gave himself up for her to make her holy, cleansing her by the washing with water through the word, and to present her to himself as a radiant church, without stain or wrinkle or any other blemish, but holy and blameless.*
>
> *In this same way, husbands ought to love their wives as their own bodies. He who loves his wife loves himself.*
>
> (Ephesians 5: 22–24)

Here, Paul shows that he believes a man should have the role of the leader in a marriage. It should be like the relationship between Christ and the Church; it is not entirely clear what Paul means by this, but clearly he thinks that the man should have authority over the woman, who should serve him. This does not mean that the man can bully his wife, or expect her to do all the work; he has to respect her, and treat her with love just as Christ loves the church. But, according to Paul, she should do as he says, and see him as an authority. This view is reflected in some versions of the Christian marriage service, where the bride can promise to obey her new husband, although he does not promise to obey her.

Other Christians believe that these views are too old fashioned for the modern world. The Bible was written a long time ago, and society was very different then. Many modern women no longer promise to obey their husbands as part of their marriage vows, and it is considered quite unusual if this is included in a church wedding. Many believe that men and women should have equal opportunities in the home and at work. They say that a couple should share care for the children and housework, and that they should both be able to go out to work if they want to. If there is a disagreement, it does not always have to be the man who has the final say.

Christians might support this view by drawing attention to verses in the Bible which are about everyone having value as being made 'in the image of God'. In particular, they might point out a verse in the letter to the Galatians:

> *There is neither Jew nor Greek, slave nor free, male nor female, for you are all one in Christ Jesus.*
> (Galatians 3: 28)

In this passage, Paul says that now they have become Christians, people should stop looking at differences between one person and another, and should recognise that they are all united. This verse could be interpreted to mean that Christians should not emphasise the differences between men and women, but should consider them as equals; in the home, this could mean that they should share work and share authority.

Many Christians believe that parents should share childcare and housework, and that mothers as well as fathers should be able to go out to work

LOOK UP

1 Peter 3: 1– 2, and verse 7

IN YOUR NOTES

(a) What does this passage give as a reason for wives accepting the authority of their husbands?

(b) How are husbands told to treat their wives?

(c) Some Christians might believe that it is still important for wives to be obedient to their husbands – others might disagree. What reasons might be given on each side of the argument?

FOR DISCUSSION

Do you think that it is acceptable for a Christian to allow an elderly relative to live in a hospital or nursing home, if they cannot manage independently? Or does a Christian have a duty to welcome elderly relatives into his or her own home, however difficult that might be?

Caring for relatives is an important responsibility for Christians

THE ROLES OF CHILDREN AND PARENTS

The Bible teaches that children should treat their parents with honour and respect. They should consider their parents' wishes and feelings, and be obedient:

> *Honour your father and your mother, so that you may live long in the land the LORD your God is giving you.*
>
> (Exodus 20: 12)

Adults have a responsibility towards elderly members of the family, and should make sure that they receive all the care they need:

> *If anyone does not provide for his relatives, and especially for his immediate family, he has denied the faith and is worse than an unbeliever.*
>
> (1 Timothy 5: 8)

Parents, too, have responsibilities towards their children. They should teach them about their faith, and expect them to be well-behaved:

> *Discipline your son, and he will give you peace; he will bring delight to your soul.*
>
> (Proverbs 29: 17)

but they should not be too hard on them:

Children, obey your parents in everything, for this pleases the Lord.

Fathers, do not embitter your children, or they will become discouraged.

(Colossians 3: 20–21)

The Bible, then, teaches that members of families have special responsibilities towards each other and it draws attention to the harm which can be caused when family members treat each other badly.

There are stories about brothers who have murderous feelings towards each other when jealousy and rivalry are allowed to go too far, for example the story of Cain and Abel in Genesis 4, and the story of Joseph and his brothers (Genesis 37). In the story of David and Bathsheba (2 Samuel 11–12), David commits adultery, which also leads to disaster. These and other stories show that families do have conflicts and tensions; brothers and sisters have always felt competitive, and married people have always felt tempted by the attractions of others, but the stories show what can happen to families if these feelings are not kept under control.

In contrast, there are stories of family love and loyalty, such as in the book of Ruth; and there is a beautiful passage in the book of Proverbs, where the writer recognises what a privilege it is to be married to a good woman:

A wife of noble character who can find? She is worth far more than rubies.

Her husband has full confidence in her and lacks nothing of value.

She brings him good, not harm, all the days of her life.

She selects wool and flax and works with eager hands.

She is like the merchant ships, bringing her food from afar.

She gets up while it is still dark; she provides food for her family and portions for her servant girls.

She considers a field and buys it; out of her earnings she plants a vineyard.

She sets about her work vigorously; her arms are strong for her tasks.

She sees that her trading is profitable, and her lamp does not go out at night.

In her hand she holds the distaff and grasps the spindle with her fingers.

She opens her arms to the poor and extends her hands to the needy.

When it snows, she has no fear for her household; for all of them are clothed in scarlet.

She makes coverings for her bed; she is clothed in fine linen and purple.

Her husband is respected at the city gate, where he takes his seat among the elders of the land.

She makes linen garments and sells them, and supplies the merchants with sashes.

She is clothed with strength and dignity; she can laugh at the days to come.

She speaks with wisdom, and faithful instruction is on her tongue.

She watches over the affairs of her household and does not eat the bread of idleness.

Her children arise and call her blessed; her husband also, and he praises her:

'Many women do noble things, but you surpass them all.'

(Proverbs 31: 10–29)

According to the Bible, Christians should try to treat everyone, even strangers, as if they were family members. They should not save their love and concern just for people who are related to them, but they should remember that everyone has equal value to God and should show Christian love (agape) to everyone they meet:

Whoever does God's will is my brother and sister and mother.

(Mark 3: 35)

Do not rebuke an older man harshly, but exhort him as if he were your father. Treat younger men as brothers, older women as mothers, and younger women as sisters, with absolute purity.

(1 Timothy 5: 1–2)

DIVORCE

Although marriage is valued very highly by Christians, not all marriages are happy. Very few marriages exist where both partners agree totally about everything, and have the same tastes, the same interests, the same attitudes towards money and the same opinions on every subject. Quarrels and misunderstandings are a normal part of married life, but in a successful marriage usually they are resolved, and the couple learn to tolerate each other even when they disagree.

Arguments are normal in married life, but sometimes a couple decide they do not want to stay married

However, in some cases, a husband and wife realise that they are making each other so unhappy that they decide to separate. If there seems to be no chance that the couple will ever want to live together again, this is known as 'irretrievable breakdown of marriage'. Marriages can run into difficulty for many reasons:

- One or both of the partners might meet someone else to whom they feel strongly attracted, and they might begin an affair. They might decide that they would rather live with this new person; or the other partner might find out about the affair and be so

hurt that they feel the trust in the marriage has been lost forever.

- Money can be the cause of many disagreements. If one partner likes to be cautious with money and feels uncomfortable without savings, while the other enjoys spending everything that is earned and does not mind having debts, then serious arguments can happen.

- False expectations sometimes cause problems in a marriage. Some people expect that marriage will involve living happily ever after, and they find it very hard to cope if everything is not perfect.

- Children can be a great bonus to a marriage – they give their parents a very special interest to share. But sometimes, children can also be the cause of conflict in a marriage. Their needs sometimes mean that the husband and wife have less time for each other, and parents might have different ideas about how the children should be brought up and what rules should be made.

- Sometimes, people just change as they grow older, and they might not have as much in common as they once did.

Whatever the reasons, it is always difficult when a marriage fails and people's expectations are disappointed. It is particularly hard when there are children, who have to get used to having two different homes and who often have to try to keep a relationship with both parents without taking sides.

DIVORCE AND THE LAW

If a couple have been living apart for some time, and they agree that they do not want to stay married to each other, they might decide to apply for a divorce. In the past, divorce was only allowed if one partner could prove that the other had committed adultery or was cruel. In 1969 the law was changed so that couples could be divorced if the marriage had irretrievably broken down, and this means that people no longer have to persuade a judge that each other is to blame for the problem. This is meant to help people to end a marriage more peacefully.

Some people think that divorce has become too easy, and that it encourages couples to take their marriages less seriously.

FOR DISCUSSION

Do you think that people would try harder to make their marriages work if divorce became more difficult?

BIBLICAL TEACHING ABOUT DIVORCE

In the Old Testament law, divorce is allowed. Nothing is said about what might happen if a woman wanted to divorce her husband, but if a man wanted a divorce, then he had to give the woman notice in writing:

> If a man marries a woman who becomes displeasing to him because he finds something indecent about her, and he writes her a certificate of divorce, gives it to her and sends her from his house …
>
> (Deuteronomy 24: 1)

However, the teaching given by Jesus in the New Testament is different. There is a passage in Mark's Gospel which describes how Jesus is asked a direct question about divorce by the Pharisees:

> Some Pharisees came and tested him by asking, 'Is it lawful for a man to divorce his wife?'
>
> 'What did Moses command you?' he replied.
>
> They said, 'Moses permitted a man to write a certificate of divorce and send her away.'
>
> 'It was because your hearts were hard that Moses wrote you this law,' Jesus replied.
>
> 'But at the beginning of creation God "made them male and female.
>
> For this reason a man will leave his father and mother and be united to his wife, and the two will become one flesh." So they are no longer two, but one.

> Therefore what God has joined together, let man not separate.'
>
> When they were in the house again, the disciples asked Jesus about this.
>
> He answered, 'Anyone who divorces his wife and marries another woman commits adultery against her. And if she divorces her husband and marries another man, she commits adultery.'
>
> (Mark 10: 2–12)

The answer given by Jesus here is very clear: divorce is never allowed and marriage is for life. The Old Testament law is made stricter.

But in Matthew's Gospel, Jesus is shown giving a slightly different view:

> It has been said, 'Anyone who divorces his wife must give her a certificate of divorce.'
>
> But I tell you that anyone who divorces his wife, except for marital unfaithfulness, causes her to become an adulteress, and anyone who marries the divorced woman commits adultery.
>
> (Matthew 5: 31–32)

Here, Jesus says that a man can only divorce his wife if she is unfaithful to him; so divorce is acceptable in some circumstances.

It is difficult to know why there are these two different explanations of Jesus' teaching about divorce. Matthew's Gospel is believed to have been written later than Mark's, and so perhaps when Matthew wrote his Gospel, he tried to make Jesus' teaching fit in better with human nature and the views of his community. Or perhaps Jesus spoke about divorce on more than one occasion, and gave these different answers because the original question was phrased in different ways. Perhaps somebody made a mistake in remembering exactly what Jesus had said.

Because the teaching of the Bible on the subject of divorce is not altogether consistent, there are different views about divorce from different Christian churches. Some believe that divorce is never acceptable, while others teach that sometimes divorce is the best solution to an unhappy marriage.

CHURCH TEACHING ABOUT REMARRIAGE AFTER DIVORCE

The **Roman Catholic Church** teaches that the sacrament of marriage binds two people together for life, and it cannot be ended; this is in keeping with the teaching in Mark's Gospel. A couple who have been married in the Catholic faith have become 'one flesh', and they stay married until one partner dies, although they are allowed to live separately. A civil divorce (one that is granted by the courts) is not recognised by the Catholic church; if the people have been married in church, then they remain married in the eyes of God. However, in serious circumstances the marriage can be dissolved, for example if only one partner is a Catholic and the other partner will not allow him or to her follow the Catholic faith. Problems such as domestic violence or alcoholism do not count as reasons for dissolving a marriage.

Another possibility for Catholics is that the marriage can be annulled. This is different from a divorce; an annulment is when it is agreed by the Catholic church that the marriage was never a real marriage in the first place. There are several different circumstances in which an annulment could be granted:

- The couple could have been married without properly understanding what they were doing; for example if one member of the couple was not fluent in the language of the ceremony.
- The marriage might have taken place without the full consent of one partner, for example if threats had been made.
- One of the partners might have had no intention of ever having children when the marriage took place.
- The marriage might not have been consummated (the couple have not had sex together).

Getting an annulment involves a lot of serious questioning, and can take a long time. If a marriage is annulled by the Church, the couple still have to get a civil divorce as well.

If Catholics want to marry for a second time when their first husband or wife is still alive, the Catholic Church will not accept this, unless an annulment has been granted for the first marriage. Because a civil divorce is not recognised, the second marriage is seen to be the same as adultery, and Catholics who have remarried while their first husband or wife is still alive are discouraged from receiving the Eucharist.

Other Christian Churches, such as the **Church of England** and the **Methodist Church**, accept that divorce sometimes happens. A civil divorce is recognised as an end to a marriage without the Church having to be involved, and both partners are free to marry again. If someone who has been divorced wants to marry his or her new partner in a church wedding, this is usually allowed. However, they do not have an automatic right to marry in church. It is up to the conscience of the individual vicar or minister to decide whether he or she thinks that the couple is taking Christian marriage seriously enough.

CHRISTIAN MARRIAGE IN PRACTICE

Because Christians believe that marriage is part of God's plan about the way people should live, and that it is blessed by God, they might make a special effort to sustain a good relationship with their husbands and wives, and they might work to promote family life for everyone:

- They might set aside time to pray together as a family or as a couple.
- They will try and make sure that their family relationships follow the teachings of the Bible. Husbands and wives will do their best to be faithful to each other, to treat each other with respect and to keep the promises they made during the marriage ceremony. They will try to encourage their children to follow the Christian faith.
- Christians might use their vote to support candidates for Parliament who appear to believe in the importance of the family.

- They might join an organisation within the Church which gives support to families and to married couples. Some churches have Wives' Clubs or groups for young married couples, which give an opportunity for Christians to talk to others about Christian marriage and to think and pray together about overcoming difficulties in a marriage. The Mothers' Union is an organisation in the Church of England that is concerned with giving support to all aspects of family life.

In spite of its name, its membership is not restricted to mothers; members can be single or married, parents or childless, women or men. The aims of the Mothers' Union are:

Mothers' Union logo

- to uphold Christ's teaching on the nature of marriage and promote its wider understanding.
- to encourage parents to bring up their children in the faith and life of the Church.
- to maintain a world-wide fellowship of Christians united in prayer, worship and service.
- to promote conditions in society favourable to family life and the protection of children.
- to help those whose family life has met with adversity.

- commit themselves in taking a full part in the life and worship of the Church in the parish and in the diocese.
- meet and work with all agencies in their local community who share the same concerns about family life.'

Members are encouraged to:

If a Christian is a member of the Mothers' Union, he or she might: run a crèche within the church so that young families can come to services; volunteer to help the families of people who are in prison; collect donations of toiletries and baby goods for the local Women's Refuge; provide babysitting for single

ICT FOR RESEARCH

Visit the web-site of the Mothers' Union:

http://www.themothersunion.org/

IN YOUR NOTES

(a) Describe some of the work of the Mothers' Union.
(b) Give some examples of Biblical teaching which might encourage a Christian to join the Mothers' Union.

The Mothers' Union supports family life in many different ways, for example by offering childcare

Sometimes Christians support organisations such as Relate, which provides counselling for people in relationships

parents within the parish; or take part in any other activities which help to strengthen family life.

Some Christians might choose to put their beliefs about the importance of marriage into action by supporting an organisation such as Relate or CMAC.

Relate is an organisation which provides education and counselling for people who are in relationships. It began in the 1940s, during the Second World War, partly because many married couples found the experience of being separated during the war years very difficult. Men who came home on leave after serving in dangerous and often horrific circumstances did not always find it easy to go back to being the person they had been before the war, and their wives too had had many new experiences which had changed their views. Many marriages fell into problems. When Relate first began, it was called the Marriage Guidance Council, because it was for married couples, but it has changed its name to Relate to show that all kinds of people are welcome to use its services, whether they are married or not.

Relate helps people by giving them a chance to talk about their problems with the guidance of an independent counsellor. The counsellor is a volunteer who has been trained to listen to people, and to ask questions, which will help them to recognise and deal with their difficulties. Sometimes, both partners will go to a Relate counsellor together,

and they will be helped to communicate with one another and express their feelings, but will not be allowed to become violent or abusive. Often, just one person will go to Relate because the other refuses to attend, but this can still be helpful. The counsellor does not give advice, but guides the conversation so that the two people can think about their attitudes towards each other and the ways in which they could change their behaviour to improve their relationship.

It is not the job of Relate counsellors to try and keep a marriage together in all circumstances. Sometimes, a couple will ask for counselling even when they have already decided to divorce, and Relate can help them to work out the best ways of organising the divorce so that the least hurt is caused.

If people want to use the services of Relate, then they have to pay, because it does not have funding from the government, and even though the work is done by volunteers, there are still costs to meet such as the use of premises and advertising.

Relate is not a Christian organisation; it is open to help people from all kinds of backgrounds, and its volunteers can have any religious belief, or none. But Christians might choose to support it, because they might believe that it is a good way of putting into action the Christian belief that everyone is valuable and that love should be encouraged. Relate can help people to continue with their marriages and communicate with each other more successfully, and a Christian might feel that this is important because it helps to preserve God's gift of marriage.

CMAC is the Catholic Marriage Advisory Council. People who use it do not have to be Catholic, or married, because the organisation aims to help anyone in need of counselling. However, its volunteers are usually Catholic, and it bases its understanding of marriage on Catholic principles. It offers guidance for couples who are planning to get married, and gives help in understanding natural methods of family planning (see page 33), as well as providing help and support to people who are having difficulties in their relationships.

Roman Catholics might choose to support CMAC, because it works on the basis of a Catholic understanding of marriage as a life-long commitment. Its volunteers are trained to understand the teachings of the Catholic Church about marriage, sex, contraception, annulment and divorce.

PRACTICE GCSE QUESTIONS

1 (a) Describe Christian teaching about the way children should treat their parents. (8 marks)
   Remember that the question asks for Christian teaching, so you could include Biblical material and any other teaching that comes from Christians. You might want to include something about how adults should treat their parents.

   (b) How might a married couple's Christian faith affect the way in which they behave towards each other? (7 marks)
   In answers to this sort of question, try to give as many examples as you can, and make plenty of reference to Christianity. As well as writing about respect, faithfulness and so on, you should make sure that you give the reasons why Christians believe this is important.

   (c) 'The head of a Christian family should be the father.' Do you agree? Give reasons to support your answer and show that you have thought about different points of view. (5 marks)
   Notice that you are asked to write about a Christian family, so you need to be careful to refer to Christian beliefs and opinions as well as explaining your own approach.

2 (a) Describe two different Christian beliefs about remarriage after divorce. (8 marks)
   Here, you are asked to give two different opinions; even if you know more than two, you only need to choose two to write about in order to gain full marks. You could refer to the Bible, perhaps.

   (b) Explain how and why a Christian might support the work of an organisation which provides counselling for people who are having difficulties in their relationships. (7 marks)
   Notice that you are being asked to explain both 'how' and 'why'; so you should write about what a Christian might do to give support (such as training to be a counsellor) as well as the reasons for this and their basis in Christian beliefs about marriage and the family.

   (c) 'There is nothing wrong with living together and having children together without getting married.'
   Do you agree? Give reasons to support your answer and show that you have thought about different points of view. You must refer to Christianity in your answer. (5 marks)
   Remember to give reasons for each opinion you describe, and try to present a balanced argument rather than concentrating too heavily on your own point of view.

3

BIRTH AND DEATH

INTRODUCTION

Issues related to the sanctity of life, and Christian responses to these issues.
Issues related to birth control (contraception), fertility treatment (the right to a child and the use of embryos), abortion, suicide, and euthanasia.
Biblical teachings about the value of human life, and the teachings of the Christian churches.

Up until about two hundred years ago, medicine did not present people with any major moral problems. Some couples could not have children and so never became parents. Babies were born, often more than ten in the same family; if they were lucky they survived to grow up into adults, and if they had serious illnesses or accidents they died. When people came to the ends of their lives, they sometimes died peacefully and sometimes in pain; there was not really very much that anyone could do about life and death. In the Bible, there are families like Jacob's, with twelve sons, and people like Hannah, childless but desperate to have a baby, and people with illnesses who have lived in discomfort for many years, like the woman with haemorrhages (Luke 8: 43–48). It was all believed to be very much in the hands of God.

However, medicine has made enormous progress since the time that the Bible was written. It is now possible for people to control the

In the past, people did not have much control over decisions of life and death. Some people had very large families, whether they liked it or not

number of children they have, by using contraception. People who are unable to conceive can have medical help, and babies are born to women who would have remained childless if they had lived a hundred years earlier. Pregnancy can be ended safely by abortion for those women who want or need this. Serious illnesses can often be cured, and even when they cannot be stopped, the progress of an illness can be slowed so that sufferers live for much longer than they might have done in the past. People can be kept alive artificially, on life-support systems, and there are plenty of drugs available to ensure that most people end their lives painlessly.

All of these advances, along with many others, may raise moral problems, for Christians as well as for others. Issues of life and death used to be left in the hands of God, because there was no other choice. Now that we have the ability to control birth and death, up to a point, should we use that ability and make our own decisions about life and death, or should we step back and continue to leave God to decide 'the time to be born and the time to die'?

'PLAYING GOD'

Some people say that when doctors make decisions about life and death, they are 'playing God'; they say that it is wrong for doctors to make these choices, they should leave things alone and let nature take its course. This way of thinking does not provide any simple answers, however. If we always had to let nature take its course, we would not be able to use medicines at all, and many people would die even though doctors have the ability to help them. For example, if a child were diagnosed with diabetes, most people would be glad that doctors could save its life with daily injections of insulin; not many would argue that this is 'playing God' and that the child should be left alone to die. However, if someone is so badly injured in an accident that they have no hope of recovery, and people start discussing whether the life support should continue, some will say that it is wrong for the doctors to choose to end the life. So people

who say that doctors should not 'play God' are really saying that in *some* situations, doctors should not interfere; but this does not really solve the problem of knowing which situations these are.

Often, doctors have to make these difficult choices, because it is part of their job. If a premature baby is born with serious problems, the doctors have to decide how hard to struggle to keep that baby alive, knowing that it will always be severely disabled. If a very elderly person has a heart attack, the doctors have to choose whether to resuscitate or let the patient die naturally. Sometimes these choices have to be made quickly and under pressure from relatives.

Christians believe that it is important for people to use medical knowledge, and not just to let nature take its course every time someone is ill. In the Gospels, there are many stories that show that Jesus himself was a healer, and the Gospel writer Luke is believed to have been a doctor.

> *While Jesus was in one of the towns, a man came along who was covered with leprosy. When he saw Jesus, he fell with his face to the ground and begged him, 'Lord, if you are willing, you can make me clean.'*
>
> *Jesus reached out his hand and touched the man. 'I am willing,' he said. 'Be clean!' And immediately the leprosy left him.*
>
> (Luke 5: 12–13)

Christians, then, see medicine as something positive, and healing is believed to come from God. However, Christians also believe that some aspects of medicine raise moral problems, and they do not always agree about the right answers to these problems.

FOR DISCUSSION

Do you think that there are times when a doctor should not interfere with decisions about life and death?

This painting shows the creation of Adam, made 'in the image of God'

THE SANCTITY OF LIFE

Christians often say that they believe in the 'sanctity of life'. When they say this, they mean that they believe there is something special and holy about life. For Christians, human life is different from other kinds of life, because in some mysterious way, people share something of the nature of God. The book of Genesis describes how God made Adam, and then 'breathed into his nostrils the breath of life' (Genesis 2: 7). In the creation story, this did not happen with the animals and the plants, but only with the humans.

Genesis also says that people are made 'in the image of God':

> So God created man in his own image, in the image of God he created him; male and female he created them.
>
> (Genesis 1: 26–27)

It is not completely clear what this means, but Christians usually understand that the Bible teaches that people are in some way reflections of God, and that in human life, something can be seen of God himself. Christians also believe that each person has a 'soul', which does not die when the body and the mind die, but which lives on after death. It is the part of the person which is judged by God, and which can join God for ever in heaven. They say that, because people have souls, they have to be treated as special; they are different from other species of animal.

Some passages of the Bible also teach that God plans each individual human life, and knows each person completely. For example, in the book of Psalms there is a piece of poetry which compares God with someone who makes a piece of cloth. If you have ever sewn anything by hand, and think about how well you knew that piece of cloth by the time you had finished your work, you will recognise what

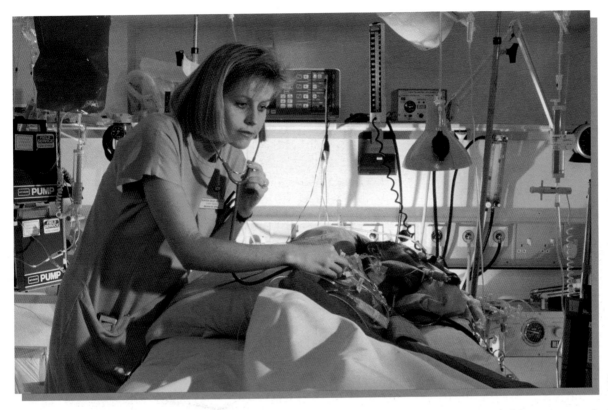

Christians believe there is something special and sacred about human life, and that God values every individual

the writer is trying to say here about the knowledge God has of each person:

> *For you created my inmost being; you knit me together in my mother's womb.*
>
> *I praise you because I am fearfully and wonderfully made; your works are wonderful, I know that full well.*
>
> *My frame was not hidden from you when I was made in the secret place. When I was woven together in the depths of the earth,*
>
> *your eyes saw my unformed body. All the days ordained for me were written in your book before one of them came to be.*
>
> (Psalm 139: 13–16)

SUMMARY

- Christians therefore believe that human life is 'sacred', it is set apart from other kinds of life.
- Other animals do not have souls, and are not made in the image of God, although they deserve to be treated with kindness and respect.

- Christians believe that God knows and plans the existence of each individual human life.

VALUING HUMAN LIFE

The belief that human life is special, sacred and holy affects Christians in many ways:

- Christians believe that God makes each person individually and deliberately, so everyone has value, whether they are newly born or very elderly, healthy or very ill, useful members of society or in need of a lot of care. This means that Christians should try to treat all kinds of human life with respect. Some Christians who choose to become doctors or nurses make this career choice because of their Christian faith: they want to put into practice their beliefs about the value of human life.

- Because Christians believe that God has given their lives to them, they think that this means they have a responsibility to take care of themselves. They should try to do something useful with their lives, rather than just waste them, and they should take care of their own health as well as the health of other people. For some Christians, this means that unhealthy activities such as smoking and over-eating are wrong, because they show ungratefulness for God's gift of life. In 1 Corinthians, which is a New Testament letter written by Paul to one of the earliest Christian churches, Paul writes:

> Don't you know that you yourselves are God's temple and that God's Spirit lives in you?
>
> (1 Corinthians 3: 16)

Christians used to believe that suicide was a terrible sin, because it showed a deliberate rejection of God's gift of life. Today, people understand a lot more about the kinds of depression and other problems that sometimes lead to suicide, and now Christians usually recognise that people commit suicide because of unhappiness rather than wickedness.

Belief about the sanctity of life affects the ways in which Christians approach medical issues such as contraception, abortion and euthanasia. However, not all Christians have the same responses to these issues.

CONTRACEPTION (Birth Control)

Contraception, sometimes known as birth control, is one area which can cause disagreements amongst Christians. In the past, couples who were able to have children had very little control over how many were born or how far apart the births were. Many families had ten or more children, perhaps one each year, and there was little anyone could do about this even if the frequent pregnancies were having a bad effect on the mother's health and the finances of the family. Today it is possible for people to decide how many children they would like to have, and when to have them, through the use of contraception.

People today can choose how many children to have and the age gaps between them, by using birth control

THE TEACHING OF THE ROMAN CATHOLIC CHURCH

Some Christians, particularly Roman Catholics, believe that artificial contraception is wrong. By 'artificial' contraception, they mean any kind of birth control which relies on more than the female body's natural menstrual cycles. For example, the Pill and condoms are 'artificial' methods of contraception, but choosing to have sex only at times of the month when the woman is at her least fertile is 'natural'.

Roman Catholics believe that sex was designed by God for a purpose: it is intended to take place only between a man and a woman who are married to each other, and it is meant for reproduction. Roman Catholics believe that this is a 'natural law'. If God made something for a reason, then people should use it for the right purpose. Roman Catholics believe that sex is spoiled if it is not an expression of love between married people, or if there is no chance of children being conceived. Natural methods of contraception are not very reliable, and so if they are used there is always the chance that a child might be conceived, if this is what God plans.

Roman Catholics usually feel especially strongly about methods of contraception which allow an egg to be fertilised, but prevent it from growing and developing, because in their view this is destroying human life and is the same as abortion.

In 1968, Pope John Paul VI issued a statement called 'On Human Life' (*Humanæ Vitæ*). He did this because during the 1960s, contraception was becoming increasingly popular and easy to obtain, and he felt that it was necessary for members of the Roman Catholic church to have some guidance about its use. *Humanæ Vitæ* stressed the importance for Catholics of traditional teachings about limiting family size using only natural methods.

THE TEACHING OF OTHER CHRISTIAN CHURCHES

Other Christian churches, such as the Church of England (Anglican), the Methodists, the Baptists and the United Reformed Church, disagree with the Roman Catholic church on the subject of contraception. Their members believe that it is a responsibility of adults to decide when to have children, if at all, how many to have and the age gaps in between them. According to these churches, using contraception is sensible and should be encouraged, because children are more likely to be loved and cared for properly if their parents want them and can afford to bring them up well.

Some churches teach that it is sensible to limit the size of a family, so that parents can afford to give their children time and occasional treats

FERTILITY TREATMENT AND THE 'RIGHT TO A CHILD'

Fertility treatment is used when people want to have children, but are unable to conceive naturally. Usually this is because of some kind of medical problem, but occasionally people seek fertility treatment because they are in a homosexual relationship, or they are not in a relationship at all but they still want to have children, or they have passed the natural age for child-bearing but they still want to have a baby.

Fertility treatment can take many different forms, depending on the problem that is preventing conception happening naturally. The man might not be producing enough sperm, for example, or the woman might not be ovulating. Sometimes, drugs can be used to overcome these problems. Often, conceiving a baby is much more difficult, and many couples who are keen to have families try many methods of fertility treatment in the hope that something will be successful. For some, this means waiting for months or even years.

Sometimes a pregnancy can be created using IVF which is 'in vitro' or 'in glass' fertilisation. IVF involves the egg and the sperm being brought together outside the woman's body, in a test tube, and then if conception takes place and an embryo is formed, the embryo is carefully placed back inside the woman's body in the hope that it will continue to grow.

Another method of fertility treatment is Artificial Insemination. Sperm is collected and placed in the woman's uterus artificially. Sometimes, this is the husband's sperm, (AIH), but if the husband is unable to produce healthy sperm, or if the woman does not have a male partner, sperm can be used which comes from an anonymous donor (AID).

IVF, and other forms of fertility treatment, do not always work, and they can be very expensive procedures. However, if they do work and a baby is born, people can become parents and experience all the pleasures of bringing up their children.

DIFFERENT OPINIONS

Some Christians believe that fertility treatments such as IVF and AI are always to be encouraged, because they bring so much happiness to people who would otherwise not be able to have children. They might say that life comes from God, and therefore anything that creates new life has to be good. In Genesis, God tells Adam and Eve to 'Be fruitful and increase in number' (Genesis 1: 28), and Christians might interpret this as a sign that God wants them to have children. They might consider the principle of agape, and the Golden Rule, and think about how they would like to be treated, if they were in the situation of being desperate to have a baby. This might lead them to the conclusion that the most loving action is to offer medical help and put to good use the gifts of healing that God has given.

Other Christians might believe that fertility treatment is wrong. They might believe that God chooses whether people have babies or not, and that sometimes God chooses some people to remain childless, perhaps so that they can devote their lives to other kinds of Christian work. They might say that it is unnatural to bring a child into the world through any other means than sexual intercourse.

Many Christians hold the view that the right answer is somewhere in between these two positions; fertility treatment can often be a good thing, but in some circumstances it could be wrong.

One of the areas that causes problems is IVF, because when scientists try to create an embryo which will grow properly in the mother's uterus, they often fertilise several eggs at a time, to maximise the chances of a successful pregnancy. This creates 'spare' embryos, and it is then difficult to know what to do with them. Sometimes they are thrown away. Sometimes they are frozen, and they can be used later for future pregnancies; sometimes they are used for important medical research in the attempt to find out new ways of improving health and overcoming disability. People might believe that it is wrong to use embryos as 'spares'; they might think that life begins as soon as the embryo is conceived, and that it should not be experimented on or disposed of, when it cannot give consent. It is the same thing as killing human life.

Other people are worried about some aspects of Artificial Insemination. When the sperm of the husband can be used in the process, the baby who is created shares the genes of both the mother and the father, just as if it had been conceived naturally. But if the sperm comes from a donor, then the baby has some of its mother's genes and some from the donor, but none from the father. Some people think that this is wrong, because it is like adultery, introducing a third adult into the marriage when it is supposed to be between two people only. They believe that this is unnatural, and that it could cause problems for the child in later life.

People are also concerned because fertility treatment makes it possible for women to have babies when they have passed the menopause, and it is possible for lesbian couples to conceive children. Some people believe that this is wrong because it is unnatural; they think that babies are meant to be born to heterosexual couples who are under fifty years of age, and they argue that it is unfair to bring a child into the world without thinking about the kind of life it will have in these circumstances.

Many believe that people should not act as if they have a right to have a child. Children, they argue, are a gift from God, and a privilege, but not something that we can demand. Other people, however, say that infertility is a medical problem, like short-sightedness, and that if doctors can do something to treat it and help them overcome the problem, then they have a right to expect this treatment.

Fertility treatment can bring great happiness to people, but some Christians are worried about aspects of it

CHURCH TEACHING

The different Christian denominations have different views about fertility treatment. For example, the Roman Catholic Church and the Methodist Church have different beliefs about what should happen to the 'spare' embryos created during IVF treatment:

The Roman Catholic Church recognises that couples who are unable to have children can become very unhappy. However, the Church teaches that human embryos are human lives, and must not be treated as if they are disposable. It also teaches that AIH is acceptable, but that AID is wrong because it introduces a third person into the marriage partnership.

The Methodist Church believes that it is right for scientists to try to learn more about causes and cures of infertility. It accepts that using 'spare' embryos for medical research is important, and believes that this experimentation should be allowed, but only in the early stages, up to fourteen days after fertilisation. The Methodist Church is keen to be involved in committees which discuss the morality of new medical investigations.

FOR DISCUSSION

Do you think that everyone who wants to have a baby should have the right to be given fertility treatment?

ABORTION

An abortion is when a foetus is expelled from its mother's uterus before the pregnancy reaches 'full term' (usually 40 weeks). Sometimes, this happens naturally, through no choice of the parents or doctors, and it is called a 'miscarriage', or a 'spontaneous abortion'. When people talk about abortion, however, they usually mean 'procured abortion', which is when the foetus is removed and the pregnancy is ended deliberately.

Procured abortions usually happen in the very early stages of pregnancy, within the first three or four months. It is safer for the woman's health if the pregnancy is not too far advanced, and also she might want to have an abortion before it becomes too obvious to everyone else that she is pregnant. In rare cases, abortions are carried out later in the pregnancy; sometimes, because the mother is very young and is too frightened to tell other people that she is pregnant until they notice for themselves; sometimes, it is because as the foetus grows, serious health problems for the mother or the foetus are discovered, and it is decided that an abortion is the best choice. Procured abortion is against the law once the foetus has been developing for 24 weeks, because after this time, if it is born it could survive.

There are many reasons why people might choose to have an abortion, including:

- The woman might not be in a serious relationship when she becomes pregnant, or the father might not want to stay with her when he discovers that she is pregnant, and she might not want to bring up the baby on her own.
- The pregnancy might happen at an inconvenient time for the woman, perhaps when she is very young, a student, in the important stages of her career, or when her other children are in their teens.
- Medical tests might show that the foetus is not developing normally, and that if the baby is born it will have serious health problems.
- The pregnancy might be the result of rape.
- The pregnancy might put the woman's health at risk if it continues.
- The woman might feel that she just does not want to have the baby, even if she could probably cope.

Some people believe that a woman should have the right to choose whether or not to have an abortion, whatever her reasons. She should not have to persuade someone else that she is making the right choice; it is her body, and she should be able to decide whether or not she wants to continue with a pregnancy. These people are described as being 'pro-choice'; they do not like being described as 'pro-abortion', because they do not want to encourage abortion. What they do want to encourage is a feeling that a woman should be allowed to make her own choice and

FOR DISCUSSION

Do you think that some of these reasons for having an abortion are better than others? Give reasons for your answer.

should not be put under pressure or made to go through with a pregnancy against her wishes.

Other people think that the reasons for wanting the abortion are very important and should be discussed with the father and with doctors, before any decision is made. Some reasons might be considered stronger than others; if a woman wants an abortion because the pregnancy would kill her, or because the baby has such a serious medical condition that it cannot possibly survive, these reasons might be seen as more important than those of a woman who just does not feel that the time is right for a baby.

According to the law, a woman cannot choose to have an abortion without a good reason. She should persuade two doctors that her mental or physical health would be at risk if she went through with the pregnancy, or that any children she might already have would suffer if she had another baby. In many cases, this just means that she tells the doctors that having the baby would cause her anxiety and depression, and this is accepted. Doctors and nurses do not have to agree with abortion, or agree to take part in caring for someone who chooses to have an abortion. If they want to, they can choose to have nothing to do with it, and different medical staff will do the work instead.

If a woman wants to have an abortion, she has to explain her reasons to doctors

ABORTION AND THE SANCTITY OF LIFE

Some of the discussion surrounding abortion depends on whether a foetus is thought to be a person or not. Christians who think that abortion is murder believe that the foetus is a person, with the same rights and the same value to God as a child who has already been born. However, others believe that the foetus is not yet a person, and so its life is not sacred. They might talk about the foetus as a 'potential person' instead. Sometimes, people say that it is like the relationship between an acorn and an oak tree; the acorn is a potential oak tree, but it is not an oak tree yet. They argue that it would be wrong to kill a living child, but that it is not as wrong to end the life of a foetus which is only a potential child.

Roman Catholics believe that life begins, and is sacred, from the moment of conception, as soon as the woman's egg is fertilised by the man's sperm, on the very first day of pregnancy. It does not matter if the life only consists of a group of cells, and could not be recognised as a baby in the making; it is still a life. Many Christians from different churches agree with this point of view. However, others believe that the foetus cannot really be described as a person until later in the pregnancy, when it becomes more recognisably human. Some say it becomes a person when the mother is first aware of it moving about and kicking; this is called 'quickening' and happens at about 14 weeks of pregnancy. Others believe that it is a person when it is capable of surviving on its own, at about 22 weeks.

BIBLICAL TEACHING ABOUT ABORTION

In the Bible, there is not very much teaching which is directly about abortion, because during the time when the Bible was written, abortion was not the common occurrence that it is today. Girls were often married very young, even before they reached sexual maturity, and they did not have careers which pregnancy might interrupt; abortion was not a safe medical procedure, and there were no tests to indicate potential health problems for the mother or the foetus.

The Bible does not use the word 'abortion' or deal with the issues directly, but many Christians use the Bible to support their views.

They might point out that the Bible stresses the sanctity of human life (see page 30), where humanity is made 'in the image of God' (Genesis 1: 26) and people are commanded not to murder (Exodus 20: 13). The commandment not to murder is often taken to

mean that it is wrong to take human life except in cases of capital punishment or war.

Christians might refer to the book of Jeremiah when discussing abortion or contraception. When Jeremiah is called by God to be a prophet, he is told:

> *Before I formed you in the womb I knew you, before you were born I set you apart; I appointed you as a prophet to the nations.*
>
> (Jeremiah 1: 5)

This could be used to argue that the Bible teaches that God knows and plans every person even before they are born. Therefore some Christians say that it is wrong to spoil this plan by preventing the baby from being born, either through using contraception or through having an abortion.

One passage in the Bible explains what should happen by law if someone causes a woman to miscarry:

> *If men who are fighting hit a pregnant woman and she gives birth prematurely but there is no serious injury, the offender must be fined whatever the woman's husband demands and the court allows. But if there is serious injury, you are to take life for life, eye for eye, tooth for tooth, hand for hand, foot for foot, burn for burn, wound for wound, bruise for bruise.*
>
> (Exodus 21: 22–25)

This suggests that the foetus is considered to have the protection of the law, but that causing the death of an unborn child is not as serious as other forms of killing. The punishment suggested is a fine, and severe penalties are only recommended if there is further harm.

CHURCH TEACHING ABOUT ABORTION

Some early Church fathers thought that abortion was allowable up to 40 days after conception, because it was believed that this was the time when the unborn child received its soul ('ensoulment'). This was based on early understandings of science, and is not generally accepted now.

Today, different churches have very different views about abortion. The Roman Catholic Church teaches that it is always very wrong to kill an unborn child, at whatever stage of development, because it is a sacred human life which deserves to be treated with the same respect as any other human being. Even if the pregnancy is the result of rape, the Roman Catholic Church would not support an abortion, because the foetus should not have to pay the price for someone else's crime. Roman Catholics try to encourage women not to have abortions, but to have the babies adopted if they really cannot cope with bringing them up. The Roman Catholic Church has made several statements about abortion, for example *Humanæ Vitæ* in 1968 emphasised that 'human life is sacred', and the *Declaration on Procured Abortion* in 1974 stated that abortion is a serious

sin and that everyone, whether Catholic or not, should have a proper respect for human life.

The Salvation Army also believes that life is sacred from the moment of conception, but it does accept that abortion should happen in a very few cases, such as where the mother's life is in danger or the baby is so severely abnormal that it cannot possibly survive for more than a few days.

The United Reformed Church recognises that there is a wide range of views among its members, but it suggests that there is a difference between a foetus that is almost ready to be born, and the early stages of pregnancy. They would not talk about a pregnancy of a few weeks as if this were already a child, and they believe that sometimes abortion is necessary, although it should be taken seriously.

All of the different church denominations stress the need to provide the woman with plenty of counselling and support.

CHRISTIAN BELIEFS IN ACTION

There are many ways in which Christians who are against abortion might put these beliefs into action. For example:

- In discussion with other people, they might show that they strongly disagree with abortion, and they might explain their opinions by making reference to their faith.
- A Christian might join a 'pro-life' organisation, which campaigns against abortion, such as Life or SPUC (the Society for the Protection of the Unborn Child).
- Their beliefs about abortion might affect the ways in which they vote. Some candidates for election, particularly in the USA, make statements about their views on abortion. A Christian who disagreed with abortion might choose to vote for someone who promised to make abortions more difficult to obtain.
- They might take part in protests against abortion. For example, they might write letters to newspapers and to their MP. They might take part in marches and other demonstrations, carrying placards that advertise their opinions. They could picket clinics which offer abortions, and try to persuade the

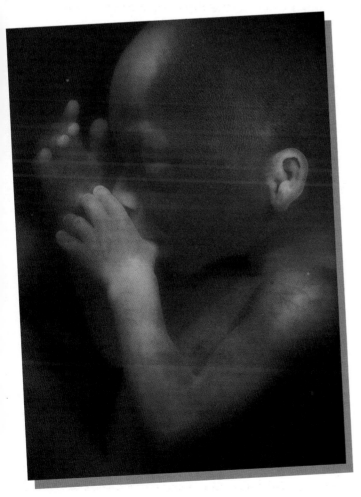

Some Christians believe that abortion is the same as murder, even though the child has not yet been born

people visiting the clinic to think again before keeping their appointments.

- They might pray about the problem of abortion, perhaps asking for God's help for the foetuses and for the pregnant woman.
- Christians might feel that it is important for young people to receive a proper sex education, so that fewer unwanted pregnancies happen in the first place. They might organise talks for the young people in their church, or work as volunteers in a counselling centre which offers help and contraceptive advice to young people.
- Some Christians believe that it is not enough to discourage people from having abortions and then leave them to get on with raising the child on their own. Sometimes abortions are wanted because having the baby is going to be very difficult, perhaps because it will be born with medical problems or perhaps because of financial or other reasons. There are Christians who, because of their faith, offer support for families in these kinds of difficulties. Perhaps a Christian might offer to baby-sit for a single parent, so that he or she can go out with their friends. Some Christians work as foster carers, and look after the children of parents who are finding it difficult to cope, on a more long-term basis.
- Christians who are offering advice to someone considering having an abortion might suggest that the baby could be adopted, as there are many couples who would love to have a child but are unable to conceive. There are various Christian adoption agencies, and a Christian who is against abortion might support one of these, encouraging women to go through with their pregnancies and give the baby to a couple who will provide him or her with a loving home.

If Christians are in favour of a woman being able to choose to have an abortion, they might put their beliefs into action:

- They might join a group which campaigns for the right to choose abortion.
- They might support an organisation which offers counselling for people who have had abortions.

- When people are talking about abortion, they might explain why they feel it is sometimes the most loving choice; they might discourage other people from harshly criticising women who have chosen to have abortions.
- They might pray about the problem of abortion.
- Even if a Christian believes that abortion can sometimes be the most sensible choice, they are still likely to believe that it is important to give people a proper sex education to avoid unwanted pregnancies happening in the first place.

THE 1967 ABORTION ACT

Before 1967, women who wanted to have abortions had to try and find someone who would perform the operation in secret; often these people were unqualified, and they could not use proper hospital premises because they would have been prosecuted. Many women were horribly injured as a result of these 'back-street' abortions, and some died. When the 1967 Abortion Act was passed, it became very much easier for women to have abortions if they wanted them, and the abortions could be done properly by qualified medical staff. By law, the woman had to persuade two doctors that her mental or physical health, or the welfare of her children, would suffer if she did not have the abortion. If the doctors agreed with her, then the abortion could take place.

SPUC – AN ORGANISATION WHICH CAMPAIGNS AGAINST ABORTION

A lot of people thought that it was very wrong to make abortion legal; they believed that it allowed innocent human lives to be destroyed and that it encouraged women to have abortions instead of looking at other possibilities, such as having the baby adopted. Some of these people joined together, in 1967, to form an organisation known as SPUC – the Society for the Protection of the Unborn Child.

SPUC is not a Christian organisation, but many Christians might choose to support it, because it campaigns against abortion and also against other issues, such as euthanasia and embryo experimentation. Its members point out that since abortion was made legal, over 4.5 million pregnancies have been deliberately ended. SPUC argues that abortion denies a basic human right: the right to life. Its members believe that life begins at the moment of conception, and that all human life is equally valuable, whether the foetus is healthy or not. They say that abortions which take place because the foetus is abnormal in some way discriminate against disabled people, suggesting that they are inferior and that the world would be a better place without them. SPUC teaches that tests during pregnancy should only be performed for the benefit of the foetus, and not in order to make a decision about whether an abortion should be carried out.

Members of SPUC raise funds to help them produce advertising material explaining their point of view. They organise protests, particularly when people suggest that the law should be changed to make abortion easier. They write letters to MPs, to try and influence them to vote against abortion when it is being debated in Parliament. SPUC also produces educational materials to be used in schools, youth groups and counselling centres, to explain to young people what abortion involves and to try and discourage young women from choosing to have an abortion.

Christians might support this organisation because of their belief that life is sacred. They might believe that it is wrong to do nothing to stop abortion, because the Bible teaches about the importance of defending the weak:

> *Rescue the weak and needy; deliver them from the hand of the wicked.*
> (Psalm 82: 4)

Their Christian faith might lead them to think that it is not enough to express opinions against abortion without doing anything positive, and they might therefore come to the conclusion that joining an organisation such as SPUC is the best way of putting their faith into action.

THE ALL-PARTY PARLIAMENTARY PRO-CHOICE GROUP

The All-Party Parliamentary Pro-Choice Group, or Pro-Choice Alliance (PCA) is a group which campaigns for the right of a woman to have an abortion without having to give anyone a reason, up to the 14th week of pregnancy. It is open to members of any religion and any political party, and it campaigns to try to change the law to make abortions easier to obtain. The PCA believes that it is wrong for women to have to explain their personal circumstances to a doctor, and then leave it up to him or

The issue of abortion raises strong feelings. Sometimes Christians attend demonstrations to publicise their views

IN YOUR NOTES

What is your own opinion about abortion? Give reasons to support your answer.

her to decide whether or not they can have an abortion. This, they say, is an invasion of the woman's privacy, and is treating her like a child, as though she is incapable of making sensible decisions by herself and needs to be told what she may or may not do by someone else, who usually does not know her very well.

Some Christians might support the work of an organisation such as the PCA. They might use the passages in the Bible which teach that men and women have equal value (see page 69), to show that women should be able to make choices about their own lives. Christians might believe that it is more in keeping with the Christian principles of love and forgiveness to allow an early abortion if a woman wants one, than to make her go through with an unwanted pregnancy and cause her suffering.

SUICIDE

Suicide is when a person ends his or her own life. It is not very common – in the United Kingdom fewer than one in a hundred deaths every year are the result of suicide – but it happens often enough for many families to have been affected by it. About three times more men than women commit suicide, and the rate among young people is rising.

There are many different reasons why a person might commit suicide. Some of them are:

- Depression, schizophrenia or other forms of mental illness where the sufferer is unable to see any hope for the future.
- Serious difficulties in coping with life, such as drink, drug or money problems, where the person cannot see any solution other than suicide.
- Bereavement, where a loved one dies and the person feels that there is no point in carrying on living.
- Bullying, where someone is made to feel so insecure and frightened that they decide they would prefer to be dead.
- Old age, when a person is unable to live independently and feels that it would be better for everyone if death came more quickly.
- Serious or incurable illness, when someone is in a great deal of pain or is deteriorating quickly, and they believe that it is better to end life with dignity than to let it drag on.
- Feelings of being under pressure, when someone believes that they are letting everyone down because they are not living up to other people's expectations.

Sometimes, people attempt suicide but they hope that they will be discovered before they die; this is often called a 'cry for help'. They might take an overdose of tablets, but not enough to kill themselves, in the hope that someone will come, realise how seriously upset they are and help them to sort out their problems.

In the past, suicide was considered to be a serious crime, and the Church treated it as a sin. If someone was discovered trying to commit suicide, they would be severely punished; and people who succeeded in killing themselves were not allowed to be buried with a Christian funeral in the 'holy ground' of the churchyard but had to have graves elsewhere, set apart from everyone else.

Today, people know a lot more about depression, stress and grief, and they are usually a lot more understanding about the circumstances which might lead someone to consider suicide. Instead of condemning the victim, more effort is made to understand and to support the relatives.

Most Christians believe that it is wrong for a person to make the choice to commit suicide, although at the same time they recognise that people who try to take their own lives have often gone beyond the stage where they are able to make sensible decisions. Christians might argue against suicide by saying:

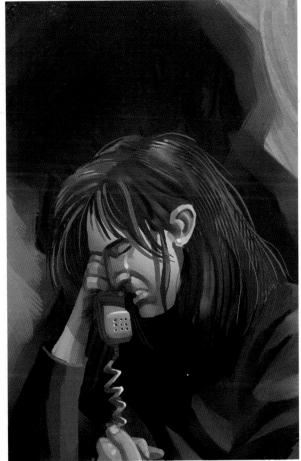

For all sorts of reasons people sometimes feel that they can no longer cope with life

- God chooses when we are born and when we die; it is wrong for us to think that we know better.
- If we suffer pain, loneliness or depression, this might be for a reason. Many Christians believe that they become closer to God through suffering, and in a way they share in the suffering of Christ. They believe that God sometimes allows people to suffer so that they learn, and suicide is a refusal to learn the things that God is trying to teach.
- Suicide is selfish, because it causes so much pain to the people who are left behind. They might be left feeling that the person who committed suicide did not care about them at all, or they might spend many years blaming themselves for the death. It is often much harder to get over the death of someone who commits suicide, than the death of someone killed in an accident.
- One of the commandments teaches 'You shall not murder'. Christians might believe that suicide is a form of murder, even if the murderer and the victim are the same person.

The most famous example of suicide in the Bible is probably the suicide of Judas after he had betrayed Jesus. When he realised what he had done, and had been given the thirty pieces of silver that he had been promised for leading the soldiers to arrest Jesus, he went out and hanged himself. The Bible does not say whether Judas was right or wrong to do this.

In a short passage in 1 Corinthians, Paul explains to the early Christians that they have a responsibility to look after their bodies, because God lives in them (1 Corinthians 3: 16). Paul compares the body to a temple, the most sacred building of all – people took great care of their temples, decorating them with their most expensive materials and considering it a great honour to be responsible for keeping the temple clean. Paul teaches that Christians should think of their own bodies like this, and look after them. Christians might use this passage in a discussion about suicide, to show that the body should be treated as a place where God lives, and should be respected, not killed.

Most Christians believe that the right response to suicide is to try to be loving and forgiving. People who attempt suicide should be helped, not condemned.

THE SAMARITANS

One organisation that Christians might support is The Samaritans. It was started by a Christian, but it is open to anyone, of any religion or none. The aim of The Samaritans is to provide confidential emotional support to anyone who needs it, in the hope of preventing suicide. It also tries to increase public awareness of suicide and depression, so that people will be more understanding and better able to help each other.

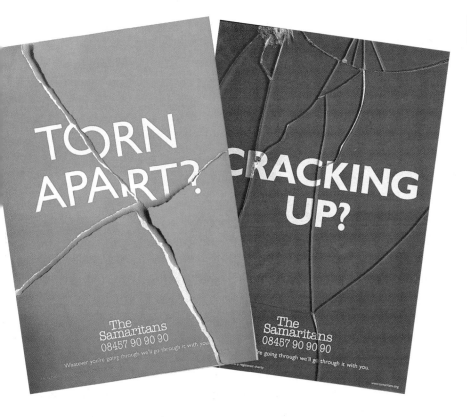

Christians might put their beliefs about the value of human life into action by volunteering for an organisation such as The Samaritans

The Samaritans was started in 1953 by Rev. Chad Varah, who was working as a vicar for the Church of England in London. When he had qualified as a vicar, one of the first jobs he had to do was the funeral of a 14-year-old girl, who had taken her own life. It turned out that this was because she had started her periods, and did not know what was happening to her; she thought she had a disease and was too embarrassed to talk to anyone about it. Chad Varah was very upset by this, and decided that there was a need for an organisation where people could talk about their problems in confidence, not even giving their names unless they wanted to. This organisation had to be available day and night, whenever people needed help, including over Christmas.

The Samaritans has a network of volunteers on the other end of the telephone or e-mail for a certain number of hours every month. The telephone number of The Samaritans is publicised on posters, stickers and leaflets. If someone feels as if they have a problem they cannot handle on their own, or they think that suicide is the best thing to do, they can call the number and talk to someone who will listen.

The volunteers are not supposed to give advice or tell the caller what to do about their problems, but they listen, and help the callers to work out their own answers. The volunteers can come from any background or religious belief, and they are not allowed to express their own opinions or beliefs to a caller.

Today, there are many branches of The Samaritans all over the country, and overseas. There are drop-in centres for people who want to talk about their difficulties face to face; there is an e-mail service for people who would rather communicate in that way; and there are still the telephone lines. It is estimated that if all the volunteers were paid for their work instead of doing it for nothing, it would cost more than £10 million a year.

Christians might support the work of The Samaritans, even though it is not strictly a Christian organisation, because they might see it as a good way of putting into practice their beliefs about the sanctity of life. They might think that supporting The Samaritans is a good way of showing agape, unconditional love, to other people who need help. Many people who volunteer for The Samaritans are Christians (although many others are not), and they give up their time as a way of putting their Christian beliefs into action.

EUTHANASIA

The word 'euthanasia' comes from two Greek words: 'eu', meaning good, and 'thanatos', meaning death. Literally, it means 'a good death'.

When people talk about euthanasia, they mean making the choice about how death occurs. In some ways, euthanasia is related to suicide, because it is about people choosing when and how a human life should end – either their own lives, or the life of someone else who is unable to make the choice. The difference between euthanasia and suicide is that euthanasia involves more than one person. As well as the one who is dying, there is someone else who performs the killing, or provides the drugs or injection, or withholds life-saving treatment, because the dying person is unable to commit suicide alone.

Voluntary euthanasia is when someone chooses to ask for the end of his or her own life, but is incapable of committing suicide without help. This is often called 'assisted suicide'.

Involuntary euthanasia is when other people decide that it would be for the best if someone's life ends, because he or she is not able to make that decision independently. They might have been in a coma for a very long time, perhaps, or they might be only a few hours old.

Active euthanasia is when action is taken to bring life to an end; for example, a lethal dose of drugs might be given. This is against the law.

Passive euthanasia is when a decision is made to stop giving further treatment, even though death will be the result. This happens quite often. It is not always easy to say whether some of these circumstances 'count' as euthanasia or not.

Euthanasia has become a complicated problem, because there are so many medical treatments available now to keep people alive. If someone is injured so badly in an accident that they lose forever the ability to think or feel, and there is no chance of recovery, they can still be kept alive for a long time. If a baby is born with severe abnormalities, it can be artificially kept alive. Euthanasia is not just about killing, but about deciding when enough is enough; sometimes, perhaps, it is kinder and more sensible not to do everything possible to prolong life.

There are many different circumstances which might lead people to think about euthanasia. Often, the question is raised if someone is suffering from an incurable illness, which is causing pain and a loss of independence. They might think about whether they want to carry on suffering for weeks or months, or perhaps die quickly while they are still able to say goodbye to their families and friends, and before the pain becomes unbearable.

The quality of life of the patient is often one of the main issues. If someone is enjoying happy relationships with other people, can communicate, and is not in unbearable pain, then most people would agree that euthanasia would be wrong; but if the patient cannot communicate or is suffering so much that they cannot enjoy life, then some would argue that euthanasia might be the best option.

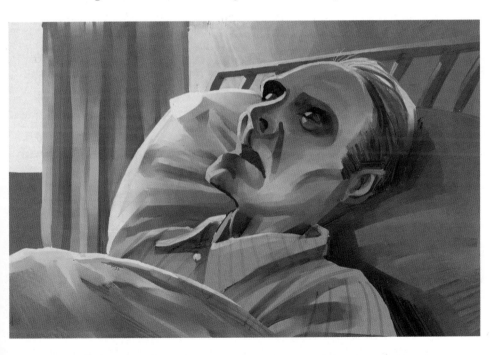

The quality of a person's life is often an important factor in discussions about euthanasia

THE DEBATE ABOUT EUTHANASIA

Some people believe that euthanasia should be legal, as a possible choice for people who want it. They say that it is unreasonable that fit people can choose to commit suicide, but that people who are not well enough for this cannot make the same choice. It is cruel to force someone to endure long suffering, when you could do something about it – most people would have their pets put down if they were suffering from an incurable illness, so why should this same kindness not be allowed for humans? The Voluntary Euthanasia Society works to change the law to allow for people to make 'advance directives'; these are statements which tell others what the patients wishes are, in case they reach a stage when they cannot speak for themselves but want to be allowed to die. The VES hopes that one day, the law will allow doctors to end the lives of people who have made it clear, in writing, that this is what they want.

Some Christians would support this point of view. They might agree that the main thing to consider is how you would feel, if you were the person suffering. You should treat others as you would like to be treated, putting the principle of agape into practice, and euthanasia could be the most loving action.

Other people argue that it would be very dangerous to make euthanasia legal. People might be pushed into saying that they want euthanasia, by relatives who do not want to look after them any more. People who are in great pain are not always able to make sensible decisions. They might change their minds, but be unable to communicate this to doctors. Many Christians would agree with this, and add that it is wrong to take away the sacred gift of human life.

CHURCH TEACHING ABOUT EUTHANASIA

The **Baptist Church** in the UK teaches that euthanasia is very similar to abortion, and raises the same sorts of issues – whether people have the right to choose to take away human life. In general, the Baptists are against euthanasia, because they believe that all human life is sacred and therefore worth preserving. However, Baptists usually agree that when a person is 'brain-dead', or cannot maintain any kind of relationship with friends and relatives, and medical experts agree that there is absolutely no chance of recovery, then it is acceptable for treatment to be stopped and the patient to be allowed to die. They do not agree with action being taken to make death come more quickly, for example by giving a lethal dose of drugs.

The **Church of England** has been involved in a lot of discussion about euthanasia in the last thirty years, and has produced reports which set out its position. It agrees that the sanctity of life is very important, but also accepts that doctors do not have to do everything possible to keep people alive, regardless of the quality of life. The Church also stresses the importance of making sure that the old and the ill are made to feel wanted and valuable, and says that the Church should do all it can to make the elderly feel important as members of society.

The **Roman Catholic Church** is totally against euthanasia, and teaches that any act which deliberately brings about death is the same as murder. However, it accepts that sometimes drugs, which are intended to relieve pain, might also shorten life, and this is considered acceptable. The

IN YOUR NOTES

Give some examples of Biblical teaching which Christians might use in a discussion about euthanasia. You could choose passages which talk about agape, or the Golden Rule (Matthew 7: 12), or the sanctity of life.

Roman Catholic Church teaches that ordinary treatments, such as feeding a patient, must always be continued, but that 'extraordinary' treatments, such as a complicated operation that is unlikely to succeed, need not be given. It emphasises that sick people need and deserve special care.

THE HOSPICE MOVEMENT

The word 'hospice' has been in use for a long time. In mediaeval times, it meant a place run by the Church where anyone could go for care, whether they were travellers, or sick, or elderly, or homeless.

Today, a hospice is a place for people who are terminally ill, and also for their relatives and friends. Hospices have expertise in pain relief; they aim to improve the quality of life for every patient. They do everything they can to make a patient more comfortable, not only coping with the major aspects of keeping severe pain under control (called 'palliative care'), but also dealing with more minor problems such as skin complaints and money worries, trying in every way to give the dying patient a peaceful and happy end to life. In this way, hospices aim to provide an alternative to euthanasia, believing that a 'good death' can be achieved without killing, if the patient is surrounded by care, love and support.

Modern hospices first began at the end of the nineteenth century, when a group of nuns set up a home in which to care for people who were dying. The first was in Dublin, and then the work spread to London. In 1967, a young nurse called Cicely Saunders helped to establish St Joseph's Hospice, which is one of the most famous. The

ICT FOR RESEARCH

Many UK hospices have web-sites, where you can find out more about the staff, the volunteers, and the work that they do. Try one of the following:

http://www.devianhouse.org.uk
http://www.boltonhospice.org
http://freespace.virgin.net/graham.leng/hospice

IN YOUR NOTES

Write a paragraph about one of the hospices you have explored, explaining what it is trying to achieve, the sorts of people it has as patients, and the different kinds of help it offers.

Hospices aim to provide a homely atmosphere, supporting patients and their relatives as death approaches

Macmillan nurses provide support and care for people who are terminally ill

work was begun by people with Christian faith; they believed that it is important that people who are dying are given the opportunity to face death positively and with dignity. However, hospices are not just for Christians, and not everyone who works there is a Christian. The staff do not try to persuade the patients to believe in God, although there is plenty of opportunity for talking to ministers or priests if this is what the patients want. Some hospices are especially for children with incurable illnesses, and the facilities are designed especially for children and their families, with play areas and gardens and room for brothers and sisters to stay.

Not everyone who is in a hospice goes there to die. Sometimes, hospices are used for 'respite care', which gives the people who usually look after the patient a break from all their hard work. Many patients spend time in the hospice until it is clear that they are going to die very soon, and then they choose to spend their last few days at home with their families, with the support of staff from the hospice. It is important that the patients are allowed to make their own choices, and do whatever feels best for them.

Special nurses, called Macmillan nurses, often visit the patients and their families in the hospice and at home. These nurses are trained in the care of the terminally ill, and make sure that the patient sees a familiar face rather than a different nursing shift every day. The hospice provides support for the relatives, as well as the patient, and care continues for the rest of the family even after the patient has died.

Some people, because of their Christian faith, choose to spend their lives working in hospices or as Macmillan nurses. Others support the hospices in other ways, perhaps by working in a charity shop which gives its proceeds to the hospice, or by other kinds of fund-raising.

PRACTICE EXAMINATION QUESTIONS

1 (a) **Describe Biblical teaching about the sanctity of life. (8 marks)**
Notice that the question asks about Biblical teaching, so your answer should stick to the Bible and not include other material such as church teaching. You need to say what the teaching is in your own words. Try to use several different examples.

(b) **Explain why Christians might support the work of an organisation which tries to prevent suicide. (7 marks)**
Notice that you are asked to give reasons why a Christian might support this organisation; it does not have to be a Christian organisation itself. You should concentrate on the reasons why the organisation fits in with Christian beliefs, rather than spending too long on background information and description.

(c) **'If people want to take their own lives, they should be free to do so.'**
Do you agree? Give reasons to support your answer, and show that you have thought about different points of view. You must refer to Christianity in your answer. (5 marks)
Remember that for full marks, you need to include a Christian view, another view (which may or may not be Christian), and your own view, each time explaining the reasons why people hold these opinions. Remember that you only have a short time to answer in the exam, so once you have covered these main points, move on.

2 (a) **Describe Christian teaching which might be used in a discussion about abortion. (8 marks)**
Notice how the question asks for Christian teaching, so you can include the Bible, the opinions of different churches, and any other teaching which comes from Christians. If different churches have different views, say what these are.

(b) **Explain how a Christian might respond to someone who asked for euthanasia to end a painful illness. (7 marks)**
Remember that Christians will have different opinions about this. Try to include the reasons why a Christian might take a particular approach: 'Because Christians believe ..., they might do ...'.

(c) **'Doctors should preserve life in all circumstances.'**
Do you agree? Give reasons to support your answer, and show that you have thought about different points of view. You must refer to Christianity in your answer. (5 marks)
You might have strong views about this, and if you can explain them well, you will score marks. But make sure that you also remember to refer to Christianity in your answer and explain another opinion as well as your own.

PREJUDICE AND EQUALITY

4

Christian understandings of issues concerning race and gender.
The work of one or more well-known Christians who have worked to overcome prejudice and discrimination.

Prejudice means 'judging before'. We often do this; we judge something before we have found out anything about it, we make up our minds before we know the facts. For example, we might decide not to go and see a film, just because the title does not appeal to us. Sometimes this does not matter. It is not usually very serious if we dislike a book on sight, without even opening the cover, or if we walk past a shop without going inside because we do not like the window display. Some kinds of prejudice are very serious, especially when it involves making up our minds about the value of other people, just because of the way they look.

Many different groups of people can be the subjects of prejudice. People with disabilities or learning difficulties are often treated as though they are incapable of doing anything at all, and as if they have no feelings. The elderly are sometimes treated as though they have nothing to offer. Homosexuals might be treated as though they and their relationships are worthless. People pre-judge – they make up their minds on first sight, before they know anything about the individuals. They are not prepared to find out the facts.

Two serious forms of prejudice are **racial prejudice** and **sexism**.

RACIAL PREJUDICE

FOR DISCUSSION

Think of some of the stereotypes that racially prejudiced people use when they talk about Jews, Asians, the Irish, gypsies, or black people.

People who are racially prejudiced believe that some ethnic groups are superior to others. They believe that the colour of someone's skin, and their ethnic origin, gives them certain characteristics, so they think that it is possible to form a judgement about someone just by looking at them. They make stereotypes of different ethnic groups, and believe that all the people who belong to that group fit the stereotype.

Racial prejudice is also known as racism – it is the belief that some ethnic groups are worth less than others.

There are several reasons why people might be racially prejudiced:

- They might have been brought up by racist parents, and learned racist attitudes from them. Very young children are not racist; they notice that a friend has darker skin in the same way that they notice another friend has ginger hair, but they do not make judgements about their friends based on this. Racism is a behaviour which is copied from other people.

In a multi-ethnic society, people of many different cultures and races live and work together. Some people are afraid of this

- Racism sometimes comes from fear. People are afraid of things they do not know much about, and if they come into contact with people who have different customs or who speak a different language, they might express their anxiety through racism. Sometimes, people who lack confidence try to make themselves feel more powerful by picking on a person or group that seems to be weaker than they are – racism is a form of bullying.
- Sometimes racist attitudes are formed in areas where there is a lot of poverty and unemployment. People look for someone to blame, and tell themselves that things would be better without ethnic minorities, and that it is all their fault. In Germany before the Second World War, the Jews were blamed for unemployment and the bad state of the economy. Today, some people blame black people or Asians for unemployment.

Racial discrimination is when people put their prejudices into action. Because of their belief that some ethnic groups are inferior, they might try to give them poorer housing, an inferior education and fewer employment opportunities. Sometimes racial discrimination involves physical harm, where people are attacked because of their ethnic origin. In extreme cases, racists try to wipe out ethnic groups entirely through so-called 'ethnic cleansing'.

Racial prejudice can lead to terrible consequences. Muslims in the former Yugoslavia were killed because of their race

Racial discrimination is against the law in the UK:

- It is against the law to stir up racial hatred by using abusive language or threats. This sort of behaviour can be punished by fines or even imprisonment in serious cases.
- It is against the law to distribute literature that is likely to stir up racial hatred.
- It is illegal to refuse someone a job just because of his or her ethnic origin. It is also illegal to discriminate against ethnic groups by withholding training or promotion.
- It is illegal to refuse to let or sell a house to someone on the basis of their ethnic origin, or to change the price because of discrimination. Hotels, swimming pools, restaurants, pubs, cinemas and all sorts of other public facilities are not allowed to give preference to one ethnic group over another.

The Commission for Racial Equality is a government body that investigates complaints about racial discrimination, and will take legal action against people who are believed to be discriminating because of racial prejudice.

This does not mean that there is no racial discrimination in the UK. There are many people who suffer verbal and physical abuse, and many people who are denied jobs or housing, just because of their ethnic origin.

RACISM IN HISTORY

Prejudice against people because of their ethnic origin has always existed, in all cultures. Whenever groups of people from one country have moved into another, there have been hostile feelings and stereotypes. For example, in the second millennium BCE, the Indus valley in India was taken over by people known as Aryans, and ancient

Aryan writings describe the people of the Indus valley as ugly, snub-nosed, and of a lower status than Aryans; these are racial stereotypes. In England in the time of Shakespeare, the Jews were stereotyped as being sly and money-grabbing. Racial prejudice has always been a way in which some people have tried to gain power over others. It has been used as an excuse for greed. People try to justify keeping a greater share of wealth for themselves, on the grounds that other people from different ethnic groups are not as important, not as human, and therefore do not deserve or need fair treatment.

The **slave trade** was an important factor in the growth of racial prejudice. From the sixteenth century to the beginning of the nineteenth, black people were taken away from their homes and packed into ships, in conditions that are illegal today even for livestock. They were sold as slaves to white families, and were treated as property. They could be overworked and beaten, and separated from their families permanently if their owners decided to sell one of them. Some of the slave-owners were prominent members of the Christian church. They justified their actions by saying that black people were not really completely human, so that Christian teaching about treating other people equally did not apply. When the slave trade became too expensive to be worthwhile for white people, it ended, and black people were free to live in countries where they had no money, no power and were still considered to be inferior.

Colonialism from the past still affects people today. Europeans thought that there was nothing wrong with interfering in other countries and taking control of them

Colonialism was another important factor in racism. Europeans such as the French, the Dutch, the English and the Germans built empires, going into countries far away and taking them over. They imposed their own government on the people, with themselves in the most privileged positions, and took away the wealth for their own use. They tried to change the customs of the people, making them eat with a knife and fork, wear more 'respectable' clothes, and convert from their own religions to Christianity. The Europeans also took with them diseases such as measles which were previously unknown. The local people had not built up immunity to these diseases and the effect was often disastrous; for example huge numbers of North American Cherokee Indians died of smallpox as a result of their contact with British and French colonists. Children in Europe were brought up to feel proud of the Empire and the ways in which so-called 'barbaric' nations were being 'civilised'.

Jessica Mitford, one of the daughters of Lord Redesdale, describes the way in which her mother introduced her to history in the 1920s:

'Muv taught English history from a large illustrated book called *Our Island Story*, with a beautiful picture of Queen Victoria as its frontispiece. 'See, England and all our Empire possessions are a lovely pink on the map,' she explained.

(*Hons and Rebels*, Jessica Mitford)

Most of the empire builders genuinely believed that they were doing the right thing. They considered that European ways were obviously better than the ways of people in other countries. They called them 'savages' and 'heathens', and thought that they were doing them a favour by imposing Western ideas on them.

THE EFFECTS OF HISTORY ON RACISM TODAY

The world today is still suffering from the effects of slavery and colonialism. People no longer buy and sell slaves from Africa and the Caribbean, but as late as the 1960s, when there were more job vacancies than applicants, black people were encouraged to come to the UK to do the jobs no one else wanted to do, such as sweeping the roads and working on London Transport, especially on the night shift. They were given the worst housing and the lowest wages. Then in the 1970s, when there were fewer job opportunities, white people decided that there were too many black people in the UK, and started talking about 'repatriation', sending the black people back to their countries of origin, even if they had been in the UK for twenty years. The attitude remains that black people can be uprooted when their services are needed, and discarded later, without a thought for their personal dignity.

Colonialism has contributed greatly to the problems of the Developing World. The people whose national wealth was taken away by the colonists have never been repaid. The world's trade

Black people were encouraged to come to the UK when there were too many job vacancies

in gold, oil, diamonds and other precious commodities is still in the hands of white people, even though these resources are found in countries where the majority of the population is black. In the media, we are still given the impression that black people are poor and in need of assistance, while white people are the heroes who go out and rescue them. We are rarely told that the cause of the poverty in the first place can be traced back to white colonialism and the exploitation of black people by whites.

APARTHEID IN SOUTH AFRICA

In South Africa during the twentieth century, a system of government was set up which was openly racist. It began in 1948, and was known as **apartheid**.

The National Party began to govern South Africa in 1948, and it made laws that were designed to keep white people and black people apart, and to give white people privileges at the expense of black people. Although more than 70% of the people of South Africa are black, and fewer than 20% are white, the white people took most of the land for themselves and made the black people crowd into areas called 'homelands', which had poor quality housing, education and medical care. They were not allowed out of these areas into the white people's land unless they carried passbooks. There was very little opportunity for employment in the homelands, so most black people had to live away from their families in hostels in the white areas. The law allowed black people to be arrested and held in police cells without trial for three months at a time, and there are many accounts of black people having been beaten and even killed by the police.

Protests against apartheid were not allowed. If anyone tried to speak out against the government, they were dealt with very harshly. The Sharpeville massacre in 1960, for example, happened when a group of people tried to hold a peaceful demonstration against South Africa's racist passbook laws. The white police moved in and killed 69 black people, and injured 186 others. Later, in 1976, black people in Soweto began rioting, and 400 were killed.

Nelson Mandela was imprisoned for twenty-six years because he refused to accept apartheid in South Africa

Although it was against the law to organise protests against apartheid, there were many brave people who did stand up and speak out against the system. Nelson Mandela, one of the leaders of a black freedom organisation called the African National Congress (ANC), ran a system of sabotage. He was arrested and sent to prison in 1964. Steve Biko, a black man who protested against the killings in Soweto in 1976, was also arrested and died in police custody.

Standing up against apartheid was dangerous, but people continued the struggle, and eventually in 1990, after twenty-six years, Nelson Mandela was released from prison. Over the next few years, the racist laws were repealed, and in 1994 Mandela was elected President of South Africa. Apartheid was abolished.

Some of the people who worked against apartheid were Christians, and they became involved in the struggle because of their Christian beliefs.

TREVOR HUDDLESTON

Trevor Huddleston was a white man, born in 1913 in a comfortable middle-class family in London. When he was a child, he did not have much contact with racial prejudice, although he did remember one story:

I can remember a strange little incident, which I suppose is revealing. When I was about 12 or 13 and my father was home and we had our own house in Hampstead Garden Suburb or just near it, one evening around Christmas – the night was quite cold and dark – the bell rang and I went to the door and I saw an old Indian looking in through the glass pane. I opened the door and my father then came out and he said – not roughly, because he wasn't that kind of a person – 'No, there's nothing here for you.' I remember that incident to this day. It seemed to me a terrible thing, not only because he was black but because he was poor, and I couldn't believe that at Christmas time you could turn anybody away. And the fact that this incident has stayed in my memory so long shows that it must have meant something important to me, I suppose.

As he grew up, he became more aware of the problems of poor people in the UK. His school was involved in community work in Camberwell in London, which in those days was one of the poorest parts of the country, and he realised that there were many children who had to go barefoot and who were seriously undernourished.

When he left Oxford University, in the 1930s, there was a lot of unemployment in Britain, and Trevor became a priest. He was determined that his Christian faith should be put into action, helping the underprivileged and doing something about injustice whenever he could.

In 1943, he was sent by his Church, (the Community of the Resurrection, an Anglican monastic order), to South Africa to help a community in Sophiatown, in the middle of a poor area for black people, a few miles away from Soweto. As well as being a part of the Church, he had responsibility for looking after education for the local black children. His work began with successful campaigns for more money for schools and kindergartens, and for free school meals for those who could not afford to pay. One 13-year-old boy was in hospital for two years with tuberculosis, and Trevor Huddleston used to visit him and take him books – he was Desmond Tutu, and it was the beginning of a lifelong friendship.

Trevor soon realised how racism was affecting the people with whom he lived and worked. In 1948, when he had been in South Africa for five years, the apartheid system was made legal, and he was faced with trying to put Christian principles into action even though the government was opposed to treating black people fairly.

I believed most strongly that fighting apartheid was a moral battle against something profoundly evil. It didn't come to me through academic reading or study. It came to me through seeing apartheid in its impact on the people whom I had responsibility for as a priest.

Fr Trevor Huddleston

Trevor Huddleston put his Christian beliefs into action by devoting his life to the struggle against apartheid

Trevor Huddleston became closely involved with people who were trying to fight against apartheid. He spoke out when Sophiatown was demolished, and the people were made to go and live elsewhere; the government put him under surveillance, keen to catch him breaking the law so that they could arrest him.

One of the ways in which Trevor Huddleston worked against racism was to organise boycotts. He thought of the idea of persuading people in other countries to stop having anything to do with South Africa, so that the government would be forced to change its rules if it wanted to stay wealthy. One particularly effective measure was the sports boycott. Teams from all over the world refused to play against South African teams in many different sports, including football and cricket. The white South Africans hated this, because sport is a very valued part of South African life.

Bands refused to give concerts in South Africa, and families in the UK and other countries stopped buying South African products, such as apples, when they did their shopping. These sanctions were very effective in helping to isolate South Africa and bring about an end to apartheid; although the UK continued to trade with South Africa in spite of Trevor Huddleston's efforts to persuade Margaret Thatcher to join the boycotts.

Trevor Huddleston was one of the leading figures in what became known as the Anti-Apartheid

The sports boycott against South Africa was a very effective way of showing that racism is unacceptable

movement. He became a close friend of many of the people who were part of the same struggle: Nelson Mandela, Oliver Tambo, Archbishop Desmond Tutu and many others.

Some people said that Father Trevor Huddleston should keep out of politics, and concentrate on his religious duties as a priest, such as giving sermons and choosing hymns. But he believed that action against racism and injustice is essential for being a Christian. Because of his beliefs that all people are equally valuable as part of God's creation, he worked in the struggle against apartheid and poverty until the end of his life. He lived for long enough to see Nelson Mandela walk out of prison after twenty-six years, and to see apartheid brought to an end. Trevor Huddleston died on 20 April, 1998.

FOR DISCUSSION

Do you think that involvement in politics is appropriate for a Christian priest?

Trevor Huddleston (centre) believed that fighting against injustice is an important part of being a Christian. (On the left is George Carey, Archbishop of Canterbury, and on the right, Desmond Tutu.)

MARTIN LUTHER KING JNR

Before the Civil Rights movement, many facilities in the USA were reserved for white people only

ICT FOR RESEARCH

Visit the web-site:

www.wmich.edu/politics/mlk

Find out more about the ways in which the Civil Rights Movement organised campaigns to desegregate public schools and transport in the USA.

FOR DISCUSSION

Do you think that Martin Luther King would have achieved more if he had used violence?

From the sixteenth century until the nineteenth, black people were stolen from their homes and taken to America to work as slaves for white people. Slavery was abolished in 1869 by Abraham Lincoln, but the black people who were freed found life in America very difficult. Most white people still thought that blacks were inferior, and black people lived in poverty. White people did not want to mix with black people; they did not want to employ them as equals, or be employed by them, or send their children to the same schools, or eat in the same restaurants, or allow them to vote, or pay them the same as white people for the same work.

By the time Martin Luther King was born in 1929, this inequality and racism was still a normal part of life. He grew up as the son of a Christian minister in the state of Georgia. At home and at church he was taught that God created everyone in his own image, and he heard stories from the Bible about the care Jesus showed for all people. When he went out, however, he saw how his family and other black people were treated as though they were inferior. Although this made him very angry, he was convinced that the right way to deal with the problem was not to use violence, but to organise peaceful protests. He would not sink to the level of people such as the Ku Klux Klan, who attacked blacks, but tried to put into practice the message of the Gospels:

> You have heard that it was said, 'Eye for eye, and tooth for tooth.' But I tell you, Do not resist an evil person. If someone strikes you on the right cheek, turn to him the other also. (Matthew 5: 38–9)

When he grew up, Martin Luther King became a Baptist minister in Montgomery, Alabama. In Montgomery, it was the rule that black people could only sit at the back of buses, not the front, and if a white person wanted the seat, the black person had to get up, even if they were old or ill or pregnant. In 1955, a black dressmaker named Rosa Parkes sat on the bus on her way home from a tiring day at work, and when a white man told her to get up so that he could have her seat, she refused. The driver would not move on, the police were called, and Rosa was taken away to jail, awaiting trial. But she had many black friends who, like her, believed that it was time for this sort of discrimination to stop. The next day fifty leaders of the black community held a meeting at the Baptist church to decide what should be done about segregation on the buses; Martin Luther King, as the minister, was there. He decided to act against the bus rule by organising a bus boycott. Black people refused to use the buses at all until the rule was changed, which happened in 1956 because without the fares of the black people, the bus companies lost more than half of their income, as white people often travelled by car. This marked the beginning of what became known as the American Civil Rights movement, and from 1960, Martin Luther King was its leader.

King was convinced that the battle against racism could only be won by non-violence. Even though people bombed his house and threatened to kill his wife and four young children, he stuck to his Christian belief that hatred must be confronted by love. He organised campaigns, boycotts, marches and demonstrations, and gave speeches to huge crowds, putting forward his vision for the future of America. His most famous speech was delivered on the steps of the memorial to Abraham Lincoln, in Washington, in August 1963:

Now is the time to rise from the dark and desolate valley of segregation to the sunlit path of racial justice. Now is the time to open the doors of opportunity to all of God's children. Now is the time to lift our nation from the quicksands of racial injustice to the solid rock of brotherhood.

We must forever conduct our struggle on the high plane of dignity and discipline. We must not allow our creative protest to degenerate into physical violence. Again and again we must rise to the majestic heights of meeting physical force with soul force.

I have a dream that one day this nation will rise up and live out the true meaning of its creed: 'We hold these truths to be self-evident: that all men are created equal.'

I have a dream that one day on the red hills of Georgia the sons of former slaves and the sons of former slaveowners will be able to sit down together at a table of brotherhood ...

I have a dream that one day even the state of Mississippi, a desert state, sweltering with the heat of injustice and oppression, will be transformed into an oasis of freedom and justice.

I have a dream that my four children will one day live in a nation where they will not be judged by the colour of their skin but by the content of their character.

I have a dream today.

In 1968, when he was only 39, Martin Luther King Jnr was shot dead in Memphis, Tennessee, by a white man named James Earl Ray. The Civil Rights Movement went on.

Martin Luther King's speeches drew large crowds. He preached a message of Christian non-violence

IN YOUR NOTES

(a) Explain why Martin Luther King chose the Lincoln Memorial as the place to deliver this speech.

(b) Explain the Christian principles which Martin Luther King was trying to put into action in his work for the Civil Rights Movement.

(c) Why do you think so many white people thought that Martin Luther King was a threat to them, even though he did not use violence?

CHRISTIAN TEACHING ABOUT PREJUDICE

Although Christians do not have a very good record in the history of racism, the Bible is quite clear that it is wrong for one person to treat another as inferior.

In the Old Testament, for example, the laws given to the people include rules about the proper treatment of foreigners, or 'aliens':

> When an alien lives with you in your land, do not ill-treat him. The alien living with you must be treated as one of your native-born. Love him as yourself, for you were aliens in Egypt. I am the LORD your God.
>
> (Leviticus 19: 33–34)

The people are told that they must treat immigrants in exactly the same way as they would treat someone who was native to their country. They should think about how they and their ancestors felt when they were the foreigners. They should give the foreigner the same love that they have for themselves, as a person of equal value.

They are also told that if they employ people, they should not treat immigrants any differently from anyone else. They should not exploit them, or try to cheat them out of receiving a fair wage promptly.

> Do not take advantage of a hired man who is poor and needy, whether he is a brother Israelite or an alien living in one of your towns.
>
> Pay him his wages each day before sunset, because he is poor and is counting on it. Otherwise he may cry to the LORD against you, and you will be guilty of sin.
>
> (Deuteronomy 24: 14–15)

In the New Testament, probably the best-known teaching that might be used in a discussion about racism is the parable of 'The Good Samaritan', from Luke's Gospel. Luke was particularly interested in showing that Jesus was concerned about vulnerable people as well as those with confidence and power.

In the time of Jesus, Samaritans were considered to be an inferior ethnic group. Their ancestors had married non-Jews, and so the Samaritans were looked down upon as being mixed race.

> On one occasion an expert in the law stood up to test Jesus. 'Teacher,' he asked, 'what must I do to inherit eternal life?'
>
> 'What is written in the Law?' he replied. 'How do you read it?'
>
> He answered: '"Love the LORD your God with all your heart and with all your soul and with all your strength and with all your mind"; and, "Love your neighbour as yourself."'
>
> 'You have answered correctly,' Jesus replied. 'Do this and you will live.'
>
> But he wanted to justify himself, so he asked Jesus, 'And who is my neighbour?'
>
> In reply Jesus said: 'A man was going down from Jerusalem to Jericho, when he fell into the hands of robbers. They stripped him of his clothes, beat him and went away, leaving him half dead.
>
> A priest happened to be going down the same road, and when he saw the man, he passed by on the other side. So too, a Levite, when he came to the place and saw him, passed by on the other side.
>
> But a Samaritan, as he travelled, came where the man was; and when he saw him, he took pity on him. He went to him and bandaged his wounds, pouring on oil and wine. Then he put the man on his own donkey, took him to an inn and took care of him.
>
> The next day he took out two silver coins and gave them to the innkeeper. "Look after him," he said, "and when I return, I will reimburse you for any extra expense you may have."
>
> Which of these three do you think was a neighbour to the man who fell into the hands of robbers?'
>
> The expert in the law replied, 'The one who had mercy on him.' Jesus told him, 'Go and do likewise.'
>
> (Luke 10: 25–37)

The parable of the Good Samaritan teaches that all people are each other's neighbours

In this parable, Jesus made the point that love (agape) should not be restricted to people who share your own nationality, but should be shown to everyone. Jesus could have chosen to tell the story so that the Samaritan was the injured person, helped by a kind Jew, but instead, he made the Samaritan the hero. People from different ethnic groups are not seen as poor victims in need of help, but as dignified members of society with their own rights and positive qualities.

The letters written by the first Christians to the new Churches also teach that any form of prejudice is unacceptable.

In the letter to the Colossians, the Church is told that its members must change their ways now that they have become Christians. It is no longer acceptable for them to build up feelings of resentment against different groups of people.

> *Put to death, therefore, whatever belongs to your earthly nature: sexual immorality, impurity, lust, evil desires and greed, which is idolatry. Because of these, the wrath of God is coming.*
>
> *You used to walk in these ways, in the life you once lived.*
>
> *But now you must rid yourselves of all such things as these: anger, rage, malice, slander, and filthy language from your lips.*
>
> *Do not lie to each other, since you have taken off your old self with its practices and have put on the new self, which is being renewed in knowledge in the image of its Creator.*
>
> *Here there is no Greek or Jew, circumcised or uncircumcised, barbarian, Scythian, slave or free, but Christ is all, and is in all.*
>
> (Colossians 3: 5–11)

The new Church is told that it must not make divisions between people, but should recognise that Christ is in all of them. They should concentrate on unity instead.

Paul's letter to the Galatians gives the same message:

> *You are all sons of God through faith in Christ Jesus, for all of you who were baptised into Christ have clothed yourselves with Christ.*
>
> *There is neither Jew nor Greek, slave nor free, male nor female, for you are all one in Christ Jesus.*
>
> (Galatians 3: 26–28)

The letter of James teaches that people should not show favouritism to some members of the Church, just because they seem to be rich and powerful. It is wrong to treat some people as superior, and other people as though they do not count for as much:

> *My brothers, as believers in our glorious LORD Jesus Christ, don't show favouritism.*
>
> *Suppose a man comes into your meeting wearing a gold ring and fine clothes, and a poor man in shabby clothes also comes in. If you show special attention to the man wearing fine clothes and say, 'Here's a good seat for you,' but say to the poor man, 'You stand there' or 'Sit on the floor by my feet,' have you not discriminated among yourselves and become judges with evil thoughts?*
>
> *Listen, my dear brothers: Has not God chosen those who are poor in the eyes of the world to be rich in faith and to inherit the kingdom he promised those who love him?*
>
> *But you have insulted the poor. Is it not the rich who are exploiting you? Are they not the ones who are dragging you into court? Are they not the ones who are slandering the noble name of him to whom you belong?*
>
> *If you really keep the royal law found in Scripture, 'Love your neighbour as yourself,' you are doing right. But if you show favouritism, you sin and are convicted by the law as lawbreakers.*
>
> (James 2: 1–9)

FOR DISCUSSION

Why do you think that, in history, so many Christians have ignored this teaching?

IN YOUR NOTES

Make a summary of Biblical teaching about prejudice and equality. In an examination, you do not have to retell the whole story (unless you are asked to do so), so try to outline the main points in two or three sentences.

This teaching could be applied to issues of race and gender, as well as to rich and poor. It explains that people should not judge by outward appearances, and should not select just a few people as important but should recognise that agape is for everyone.

THE TEACHING OF THE CHURCHES

Christian churches today recognise that in the past, they have failed to show equal concern for people of all races. There have been Church leaders who were slave traders or enthusiastic supporters of colonialism. Others, however, have made a stand against racism. For example, in the eighteenth century when slavery was at its height, members of the Religious Society of Friends (the Quakers) refused to have slave owners or slave traders in their membership.

Statements from all different Christian denominations show that they agree that there is no place for racial prejudice within Christianity. They state their belief that God created all of humanity in his own image, and that therefore Christians should oppose racism. They should be against deliberate discrimination, and should also be aware of the sort of unthinking attitudes that can lead to unfairness. The Churches are also making an effort to challenge their own behaviour, by considering how they can make people of all different ethnic backgrounds more welcome in their services and more appropriately represented in their ministry.

The Church of England held a debate called 'Rejoicing in Suffering' in 1993, to talk about Africa and the Christians there. At the end of the debate, it was agreed that Christians should acknowledge the contribution made by Africans to the Church, and should try to learn from them. They said that missionary work was still important, but that its role should change into one of partnership.

Black people are still underrepresented in Christian leadership

SEXISM

Another form of prejudice is sexism, which is the belief that one gender is inferior to the other. In practice, this is nearly always the belief that women are inferior to men. Many people believe that men and women have important differences, some of them physical and some psychological or emotional. Some people think that because of these differences, women deserve to have fewer choices than men, to do more than half of the world's work for lower pay than men, and to be judged on their appearance as objects rather than as people with dignity.

Sex discrimination is when sexist attitudes are put into practice, so that women, or sometimes men, are disadvantaged because of their gender. For example, a woman might be overlooked for promotion and the job might be given to a man even though the woman might be more experienced and better qualified. Or a man might be refused a job as a nurse or a primary school teacher, because these are traditionally female roles and a prejudiced person might assume that he would not do the job as well as a woman.

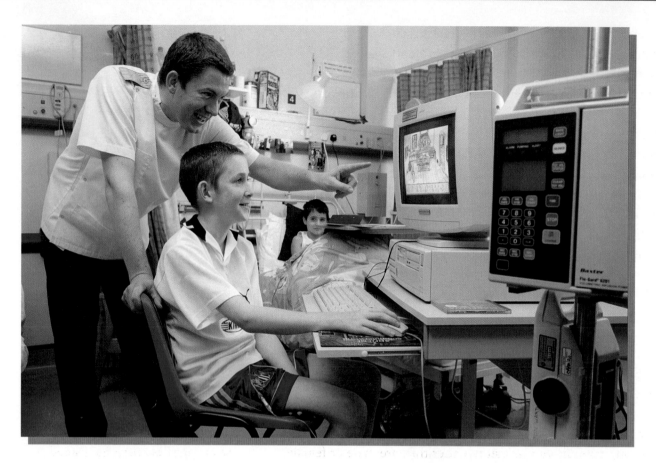

Although there are male nurses, many people still believe that caring professions are more suitable for women than for men

In the past, society in the UK has put women at a disadvantage. Before reliable contraception was easily available, many women spent almost all of their adult lives producing children and looking after them in the home. Education for girls was limited, and often concentrated on learning domestic skills such as sewing.

During the Industrial Revolution, poorer women often had jobs in factories, but these involved long hours in dangerous conditions, and women were paid less than men for doing the same work. There were very few jobs available for so-called 'respectable' women, and it was expected that when a woman married, she would give up her job straight away so that she could look after her husband.

Women were not allowed to vote until 1918, after a long struggle; and even then, voting was restricted to women who had property, or who had been to university, and were over 30 years old. It was only in 1928 that women were allowed to vote as equals with men.

During the twentieth century, two World Wars and economic reasons such as inflation meant that it became much more acceptable for women to go to work. By the 1960s, women made up 40% of the workforce. In 1975, the Sex Discrimination Act was passed, which made it illegal to discriminate against job applicants because of their gender. Employers now have to have equal opportunities policies, and they must make sure that training and promotion are available equally to men and women.

Although sex discrimination is now against the law, it is still the case that women earn less than men and hold far fewer positions of power and influence. Women represent at least half of the voting population, and yet only a small percentage of MPs are women. Women represent the majority of church-goers, but some churches will not allow women to play an equal role in church leadership.

Some people believe that it is unreasonable for women to expect to have the same kind of careers as men, because pregnancy and child-birth take up a lot of a woman's energy and attention, and they say that if women want to be mothers, they cannot expect their employers to be happy about time taken out for ante-natal care, maternity leave and child-care. Others point out that parenting should be shared between women and men, and that employers should make the effort to support family life by providing flexible working hours.

THE LEADERSHIP OF CHRISTIAN CHURCHES AND GENDER

Some Churches, such as the **United Reformed Church** and **The Salvation Army**, have always accepted women on equal terms with men in all aspects of ministry and leadership. Their members believe that if someone is right for the job of leading a local church or a national organisation, it should not matter whether they are male or female.

Other denominations, such as the **Baptists** and the **Church of England**, changed their views during the twentieth century. In the past,

The issue of whether women should be ordained as priests has caused serious disagreements between Christians

The Virgin Mary is represented as a symbol of the ideal woman

leadership was kept only for men, but Baptists began ordaining women in the 1920s, and the Church of England in 1994. Some members of the Church of England were very unhappy about this, and because they felt that it was wrong to allow women to take on the role of a priest, they left the Church of England and became Roman Catholics.

In the **Roman Catholic Church**, and also in the **Eastern Orthodox Church**, women are not allowed to become priests. These Churches teach that when the priest celebrates the Eucharist, he represents Christ, and it is inappropriate and disrespectful for a woman to take on this role. They believe that women are not inferior to men, but are different. Women have their own skills and talents which should be celebrated, such as motherhood, which has always been very highly regarded by these Churches. The Catechism of the Catholic Church states:

> *Each of the two sexes is an image of the power and tenderness of God, with equal dignity though in a different way.*

Some people think that Roman Catholic views about women's ordination and about issues that affect women, such as divorce, abortion and contraception, are old-fashioned and sexist. Roman Catholics might argue in response to this that they value the special role of women very much, as can be seen in the respect that is shown to the Virgin Mary.

IN YOUR NOTES

Write a paragraph explaining why some Christians believe that women should not be priests. Then write a second paragraph showing why others disagree.

THE BIBLE AND GENDER

(See also Chapter 2 on the roles of husbands and wives, page 18)
The Bible is not completely consistent in its teaching about gender. In many passages, it is assumed and accepted that men have more rights than women. For example, the Old Testament laws about divorce allow a man to divorce his wife if he wants to, but nothing is said about her rights if she wants to divorce him (Deuteronomy 24: 1).

Society in Old and New Testament times was **patriarchal** – men had the dominant role, and women were treated as their property. In the Ten Commandments, for example, when people are told not to envy each other's property, wives are included in a list of a man's belongings, alongside houses and donkeys:

> *You shall not covet your neighbour's house. You shall not covet your neighbour's wife, or his manservant or maidservant, his ox or donkey, or anything that belongs to your neighbour.*
>
> (Exodus 20: 17)

In the New Testament, too, women are sometimes expected to follow the orders of the men and not express their own opinions:

> *I also want women to dress modestly, with decency and propriety, not with braided hair or gold or pearls or expensive clothes, but with good deeds, appropriate for women who profess to worship God.*
>
> *A woman should learn in quietness and full submission. I do not permit a woman to teach, or to have authority over a man; she must be silent.*
>
> (1 Timothy 2: 9–12)

Some people have drawn attention to the fact that Jesus chose men as his apostles, but not women. They argue that this proves that men were always meant to be the leaders in the church, not women.

However, there are other passages in the Bible that show a different picture. For example, although some parts of the New Testament teach that women should not speak in church, in the Old Testament there are plenty of examples of women who had an important role in encouraging people to follow God. For example, Queen Esther saved the Jews from death; Ruth set an example of love and loyalty; Huldah was a very respected prophet who was asked advice by the priests. Deborah was a prophet at a time when the Israelites were fighting many battles, and her wisdom was clearly very much admired:

> *Deborah, a prophetess, the wife of Lappidoth, was leading Israel at that time. She held court under the Palm of Deborah between Ramah and Bethel in the hill country of Ephraim, and the Israelites came to her to have their disputes decided.* (Judges 4: 4–5)

In the New Testament, Jesus is shown visiting the house of Martha and Mary, and in conversation with a Samaritan woman at a well, and praising a widow for giving all she had as an offering to God. Luke's Gospel, in particular, emphasises that Jesus took notice of women as well as men. It was women who were the first to see Jesus after his resurrection:

> *On the first day of the week, very early in the morning, the women took the spices they had prepared and went to the tomb. They found the stone rolled away from the tomb, but when they entered, they did not find the body of the LORD Jesus. While they were wondering about this, suddenly two men in clothes that gleamed like lightning stood beside them. In their fright the women bowed down with their faces to the ground, but the men said to them, 'Why do you look for the living among the dead? He is not here; he has risen!'* (Luke 24: 1–6)

In Luke's gospel, women were the first to realise that Jesus had risen from the dead

These examples show that not only men but also women have played a very important part in the development of Christianity.

Christians still do not agree about the place of women in the Christian Church. Some people believe that men and women should be treated as the same in every way. They should be leaders, preachers, and priests, alongside men. They say that Christians should recognise that everyone is made in the image of God, and that at Pentecost the Holy Spirit was given to men and women equally. Women should have important jobs within the Church, and not just arrange the flowers, organise the crèche and make the tea.

Other Christians believe that although men and women are equally valuable to God, they have different gifts which should be put to different uses. They argue that it was not an accident that Jesus chose only men to be his apostles. Some roles in the Church, they argue, are more suitable for men.

Some people believe that religions such as Christianity are responsible for women having been treated as inferior in the past. They say that the teaching of the Bible, and the way that it has been interpreted by the Churches, has encouraged injustice.

CHRISTIAN BELIEFS IN ACTION

If Christians take the view that it is wrong to be prejudiced and to discriminate against other people, there are many ways in which they could put their beliefs into action. For example:

- They might make a special effort to avoid making judgements about people before they know them properly.
- If they are at work, they could do all they can to make sure that equal opportunities policies are implemented.
- They could make it clear to their friends and colleagues that they disapprove of racist or sexist jokes.
- They could try to bring up their children to share their views about all of humanity being equally valuable.
- They could pray about the problems caused by racism and sexism.
- They could join an organisation which campaigns for equality.
- They could make sure that members of the community who are from ethnic minorities are made to feel welcome, included and respected.
- They could use their votes to support a candidate whose policies are anti-racist and anti-sexist.
- They could take part in a peaceful demonstration against racism or sexism.

PRACTICE EXAMINATION QUESTIONS

1 (a) **Describe the work of one well-known Christian who has worked against racial prejudice. (8 marks)**

Remember to choose someone who has made it clear that he or she is a Christian. Martin Luther King, Trevor Huddleston or Desmond Tutu would be a better choice than Nelson Mandela, for example. Try to include something which shows how their work was influenced by their Christian faith.

(b) **Explain how Christians might use the teaching of the Bible about prejudice in their daily lives. (7 marks)**

This question asks you to relate Biblical teaching to ordinary life. So you should use some short quotations from the Bible, and some examples of what Christians might do about this. It does not matter if, in an examination, you forget where a Biblical passage comes from. If you can give the chapter and verse number that is good, but if not, just say 'in the Gospels' or 'in the New Testament' or just 'in the Bible'.

(c) **'People are not the same, so there is no reason to treat them as equals.' Do you agree? Give reasons to support your answer, and show that you have thought about different points of view. You must refer to Christianity in your answer. (5 marks)**

You might be able to use some of your Biblical examples here, to support a Christian point of view. Remember to give more than one opinion in your answer, and to support these opinions with reasons.

2 (a) **Describe Christian teaching which might be used in a discussion about sexism. (8 marks)**

Notice that this question asks about Christian teaching, so as well as using the Bible you can also include teachings from the Churches. Remember that, in a discussion about sexism, Christian teaching could be used to support more than one point of view. Show that you realise that not all Christians agree about this.

(b) **Explain how and why a Christian might work to make the world a fairer place for people of different races. (7 marks)**

To answer this question, you should concentrate on things that a Christian might do. You could include the ways an ordinary Christian might behave, or you could refer to the work of somebody special such as Martin Luther King. Try to include several different ideas in your answer.

(c) **'Christians should sometimes use violence to fight against racism'. Do you agree? Give reasons to support your answer, and show that you have thought about different points of view. (5 marks)**

Here, you might need to use some of the work from Chapter 5 on violence and non-violent protest, as part of your answer. Perhaps you could use the example of Martin Luther King's non-violent protests. Remember to include and explain your own point of view.

5

WAR, PEACE AND HUMAN RIGHTS

Christian understandings of a 'Just War'; pacifism, and violent and non-violent protest; human rights, and prisoners of conscience.

War destroys lives, homes and communities. This woman's family probably shared many meals in this kitchen; now everything has gone

The twentieth century was a century of war. Millions were killed in the First and Second World Wars, which were fought on a scale that had never been seen before. Other conflicts, too, have claimed many thousands of lives: the Vietnam war, the conflict in Northern Ireland, the wars in the Balkans, in the Middle East and in Rwanda are just a few of the hundreds of conflicts that have affected so many people. More than 30,000 people are killed every month because of war, and others too die because the leaders of their countries are spending so much on weapons that they are unable to provide clean water and adequate health care for ordinary people. The costs of war are enormous.

Christians believe that war is wrong and that God desires everyone to live in peace. However, Christians have different views about how peace is to be achieved. Some believe that it is never right to use violence, whatever the circumstances. Others argue that sometimes, war is necessary in order to overcome evil.

BIBLICAL TEACHING ABOUT WAR AND THE USE OF VIOLENCE

In the Bible, issues of war and peace are dealt with in many different ways. The Bible was not written all at the same time, but over many hundreds of years, for people in different situations. Sometimes they were at peace with their neighbours, sometimes at war; sometimes they won battles, and sometimes they lost and were taken into exile or had to live under the rule of a foreign power. These varied situations are reflected in the teaching of the Bible about war and peace, and because there are so many different teachings, Christians have very different opinions about the morality of war and whether it can ever be right to use violence. The Bible can be used to support many different points of view.

CHRISTIAN VIEWS IN SUPPORT OF WAR

In the **Old Testament**, people are sometimes commanded by God to go to war. In the books of Deuteronomy, Joshua and Judges, there is a lot about God telling the people to fight and destroy foreign tribes in order to gain possession of the Promised Land.

> *The LORD your God will drive out those nations before you, little by little. You will not be allowed to eliminate them all at once, or the wild animals will multiply around you. But the LORD your God will deliver them over to you, throwing them into great confusion until they are destroyed. He will give their kings into your hand, and you will wipe out their names from under heaven. No one will be able to stand up against you; you will destroy them.* (Deuteronomy 7: 22–24)

Later, too, the prophets sometimes tell the people that God wants them to go and fight, for example in the book of Joel:

> *Proclaim this among the nations; Prepare for war! Rouse the warriors! Let all the fighting men draw near and attack. Beat your ploughshares into swords and your pruning hooks into spears ...* (Joel 3: 9–10)

In the **New Testament**, although the message is very much one of peace, Jesus is once said to have shown anger and violence when he saw that the Temple was being used by dishonest dealers and loan sharks:

> *On reaching Jerusalem, Jesus entered the temple area and began driving out those who were buying and selling there. He overturned the tables of the money-changers and the benches of those selling doves* (Mark 11: 15)

Some Christians might interpret this to mean that it can sometimes be right to be violent when people are being cheated or treated unfairly. Also, they might point out that Jesus came into contact with soldiers, but the Gospels do not give any hint that he told them they were wrong to fight. The story in Luke's Gospel of Jesus healing a centurion's servant (Luke 7: 1–10) shows a soldier who was well respected and who was praised by Jesus for his faith; Jesus did not tell him that he was wrong to be a soldier.

Christians might use these examples in a discussion about war and the use of violence, to support the view that sometimes military action is the best way of making sure that there is justice.

CHRISTIAN VIEWS OPPOSING VIOLENCE

Not all of the Old Testament is full of war and violence; there is often a message of peace and justice. The prophet Isaiah, when he speaks about the coming of the Messiah, calls him the 'Prince of Peace':

> *And he will be called Wonderful Counsellor,*
> *Mighty God,*
> *Everlasting Father,*
> *Prince of Peace.*
> *Of the increase of his government and peace there will be no end.*
> (Isaiah 9: 6–7)

Micah, another prophet, looks forward to a time when God's rule is established, and this will be a time of peace. He deliberately reminds his listeners of the words of Joel, and tells them that things are going to change. Everything will be reversed; instead of farming equipment being made into weapons, the weapons will not be needed and can be made back into tools:

> They will beat their swords into ploughshares and their spears into pruning hooks. Nation will not take up sword against nation, nor will they train for war any more. (Micah 4: 3)

Christians might interpret this to mean that peace is a feature of the kingdom of God, and that therefore they should be peaceful themselves.

Much of the New Testament suggests that Christians should try to promote peace:

> Blessed are the peacemakers. (Matthew 5: 9)
>
> Love your enemies, and pray for those who persecute you. (Matthew 5: 44)
>
> If someone strikes you on the right cheek, turn to him the other also. (Matthew 5: 39)
>
> Do not repay evil with evil or insult with insult, but with blessing, because to this you were called so that you may inherit a blessing. (1 Peter 3: 9)

They could use these verses to support a view that violence is never acceptable. Jesus is teaching that the right response to aggression is love, and that Christians should not behave violently even when they are attacked.

Christians might also draw attention to the example of Jesus at his arrest:

> Then the men stepped forward, seized Jesus and arrested him. With that, one of Jesus' companions reached for his sword, drew it out and struck the servant of the High Priest, cutting off his ear.
>
> 'Put your sword back in its place,' Jesus said to him, 'for all who draw the sword will die by the sword.' (Matthew 26: 52)

Christians who try to follow the example of Jesus, by behaving in the way that Jesus behaved, might say that because Jesus would not allow people to use violence to defend him, this means that violence is wrong, and that peaceful methods of defence should always be used. They might refer to the Ten Commandments, especially the rule:

> You shall not murder. (Exodus 20: 13)

This could be used to argue that killing is never right in any circumstances. However, some people point out that this refers specifically to murder, and not other forms of killing, such as war and capital punishment, because these are allowed in other parts of the Bible.

Christian teaching about agape (see Chapter 1) includes the belief that love should be shown unconditionally to everyone, whether they are family, friends, strangers or enemies. It is difficult for many Christians to see how loving someone could involve killing them in a war.

Teaching about the sanctity of life (see Chapter 3, Birth and Death), where everyone is made in the image of God, also suggests that killing in a war might be wrong, because it involves taking away a life that has been made and planned by God.

Some Christians therefore believe that it is never right to retaliate or to use violence, even when other people are aggressive. These people (whether Christian or not) are called **pacifists** (see page 78).

FOR DISCUSSION

Do you think that killing in a war is the same as murder? If not, what makes it different?

DIFFICULTIES IN INTERPRETING THE BIBLE

Christians have often had difficulty understanding why the Old Testament is so full of war and violence, while the New Testament preaches agape and peace. Sometimes, they say that this is because the Old Testament people had only a limited understanding of what God was like, because Jesus had not yet come. They say that when Jesus lived in the world, he showed people the nature of God much more clearly, by healing the sick, calming the storm, raising the dead and teaching forgiveness.

Other people argue that the Bible is the word of God, and is never wrong. They say that if the Old Testament shows God ordering a war, then that is the truth about what happened. They might say that the different attitudes in the Bible are there because of different circumstances; sometimes war is wrong, but at other times, it could be what God wants.

THE ATTITUDES OF CHRISTIAN CHURCHES TO WAR

Christian attitudes to war and to the use of violence have changed during the course of history. From the earliest days of Christianity, it was believed that it was right to go to war in order to defend the innocent, or if the war was a 'holy war', fought in order to defend the religion. St Augustine, one of the leading figures of early Christianity, agreed that it could often be right for a Christian to go to war.

In the Middle Ages, Christians led campaigns known as the Crusades. Jerusalem was under Muslim rule, and had been for 400 years. The Church, with the support of the Popes, went out to fight against the Muslims and to try and recapture Jerusalem. They also wanted to prevent the Muslims from expanding their empire, and they wanted to keep and build trade routes too. These Crusades were believed, at the time, to be good and right. Some people went into the fighting because of personal greed, but many of the Crusaders believed that God was on their side, and that when they fought against Muslims and Jews, they were fighting evil. The battles were often brutal, and the treatment of prisoners was cruel, but the Christians took part enthusiastically, believing that they were fighting a 'holy war'. Sometimes the

This painting from the Middle Ages shows the artist's ideas about the Crusades. The Crusaders are shown dressed in white, a symbol of holiness

Crusades were successful; on 15 July, 1099, the Christians captured Jerusalem, and all the inhabitants were massacred. Later, however, strong Muslim rulers fought back and Jerusalem was once again lost. Christians today look back on the cruelty of the Crusades as one of the most shameful times in Christian history.

In the thirteenth century, St Thomas Aquinas decided that it was time to set out some rules, so that people could decide whether or not war should be fought. Using the ideas of other thinkers before him, he said that it was only right to go to war if certain conditions were met. This became known as the **Just War** theory. A war was just, or right, only if it matched the following:

1 War should be declared by a proper authority such as a government or a king, and not just by any ordinary group of people.
2 There must be a good reason for starting a war, not simply greed.
3 The reason for going to war must be a desire to do good.

4 War must be a last resort, when everything else has been tried first.

5 The good that is likely to come out of the war must amount to more than the harm that will be done.

6 It must be possible to win. Wars should not be fought against an opponent who is obviously much more powerful.

7 The war must be fought fairly. The amount of force used must be only enough to succeed. There must not be deliberate unnecessary cruelty.

Up until the First World War (1914–18), most of the Churches continued to support their countries when they were at war. But the killing in the First World War was on a scale that had never happened before. Nine million people died and 21 million more were seriously injured. Christians began to feel that perhaps they had been wrong to give military action so much support and encouragement.

When the Second World War began in 1939, most of the Christian churches agreed that it was important to fight against Hitler. But there were also many people who were unhappy about some of the methods used, such as the 'carpet bombing' of the beautiful German city of Dresden, which was reduced to ruins. The Allies did not seem to be aiming at any particular military target, but appeared to be deliberately terrorising civilians. Some Christians felt that this was not acceptable according to the terms of the Just War theory; they said that unnecessary force was being used.

At the end of the Second World War, the first atomic bombs were dropped on the Japanese cities of Hiroshima and Nagasaki. The effects were devastating. Thousands of people died instantly in the blast, and the radiation from the bomb killed many others. In the following months and years, babies were born dead or seriously deformed, and adults and children developed cancers. Some Christians believed that this was necessary, because it

After the First World War, some Christians began to wonder whether they had been right to support the fighting so enthusiastically

brought a swift end to the war with Japan, but others said that it was an evil thing to have done, that it was totally against Christian teaching and that it should never be allowed to happen again.

The nature of war changed completely during the twentieth century. In the First World War, nearly all the people who were killed were soldiers. In wars today, 95% of the people killed are civilians – women, children, and elderly people included. The Churches have to think about several different issues:

- Whether it is right for a Church to encourage its members to fight for their country in a time of war;
- Whether it is right for the Church to support the country if it wants to build its stores of nuclear weapons;
- Whether the Church should support people who refuse to go to war for religious reasons (conscientious objectors).

The **Church of England** today teaches that war is sometimes 'an unfortunate necessity', something which might have to happen in order to prevent even worse evil. The Church of England and the Methodist Church accept the right of individuals to follow their own consciences about whether or not to fight in a war.

The Church of England (in the 'Church and the Bomb' report of 1983) also teaches that Britain needs some kind of nuclear weapons as a deterrent, but that countries should work together for 'multilateral disarmament', where all countries aim to get rid of nuclear weapons together. The **Catholic Church** agrees, teaching that nuclear weapons must only be used as a deterrent, to prevent war, and must never be used to attack whole populations or whole cities. Countries which have nuclear weapons should always be working towards reducing them. Statements from the Roman Catholic Church and the Church of England encourage their members to pray for peace.

A modern form of the Just War theory has been drawn up, showing that the churches believe there is

Hiroshima – weapons of mass destruction have the potential to wipe out whole populations. Christians disagree about whether the country needs to have them

still a need for a set of guidelines even though the nature of war has changed so much since the time of St Thomas Aquinas. The new way of deciding whether a war is just involves the following conditions:

1 Going to war must be in defence after an unjust attack – Christians should not be the first to declare war.
2 There must be a realistic chance of success.
3 There must be some proportion between the costs of the war and the agreement made after the war – the surrendering country should not be made to pay so much money that the people who live there can never recover.
4 Only military targets should be attacked, not civilians.
5 The force used should be for a good reason.

Although there are these guidelines, Christians still do not always agree about them in practice. For example, there might be disagreement about whether the reason for wanting to use force is good or not; and often, during wars, decisions have to be made quickly, and there is not the time for lengthy debates.

Since the Second World War, Churches have been involved in discussions about the use of chemical weapons, and have been a part of the campaign to ban the use of landmines.

Many Christian churches, then, hold the view that although war is wrong, it can sometimes be the only way of resolving a situation. They argue that Christians have a responsibility to defend the weak, and that it would be wrong for a Christian to stand aside and do nothing if others are suffering because of the aggressive actions of another country.

PACIFISM

The **Religious Society of Friends**, usually known as the Quakers, takes a different view. Quakers believe that war can never be justified. They recognise that there is evil in the world, but they say that evil cannot be overcome with the use of weapons which

harm and kill. They believe that Christians should use 'weapons of the Spirit' – love, truth, peace – to overcome evil. Quakers are against the possession and use of nuclear weapons. People who hold these views, whether they are Quakers or not, are known as **pacifists.**

Quakers, and other pacifists, point out that pacifism is not the same as doing nothing to resist evil. Pacifists do fight against injustice and aggression, but in a non-violent way.

People who are firmly opposed to any form of warfare in any circumstances are called, in times of war, **conscientious objectors** – their consciences tell them to object to war. During a war, they refuse to fight as soldiers or work in the production of arms, but instead aim to promote peace in other ways such as nursing or carrying stretchers or driving ambulances.

Not all pacifists are Christian, but Christians might decide to be pacifists because of the teaching in the Bible that emphasises peace (see pages 73–74). The decision to deploy US Cruise Missiles in Western Europe in the early 1980s was very controversial, and led to a huge growth in the 'peace movement' and a new interest in the Campaign for Nuclear Disarmament (CND). A former Roman Catholic priest, Mgr Bruce Kent, its General Secretary, became a familiar figure on radio and television, encouraging people to support the campaign for getting rid of nuclear weapons.

IN YOUR NOTES

(a) Explain, using Biblical examples, why some Christians believe that going to war is sometimes necessary.
(b) Explain what 'pacifism' is. Using different Biblical examples, explain why some Christians are pacifists.

NON-VIOLENT PROTEST
Some Christians and non-Christians believe that non-violent protest is the best response to aggression, violence and injustice in all circumstances. They

believe that whatever happens, violence should not be used as a response. Non-violent protest is not the same as doing nothing. It can take many different forms, including marches and demonstrations, boycotts, sit-ins, and the use of the vote. However, in some situations, some of these methods are not possible without great risk. In some countries, not everyone has the right to vote in a fair election, and people who try to make a protest are attacked by the police.

Martin Luther King (see page 60), for example, believed that it was wrong to use violence against racism. Even though he was treated violently, he responded by using speeches, boycotts, sit-ins and other forms of peaceful protest. He believed that using violence makes the victim as bad as the attacker. He thought that it was more important to keep self-respect and use non-violent protest, even when his life was in danger.

Non-violent protest is not necessarily cowardly. This Chinese student chose to protest against his government in Tiananmen Square

FOR DISCUSSION

Do you think that non-violent protest can work? Why do some people prefer non-violent protest even when they are being treated violently?

HUMAN RIGHTS

In 1948, after the Second World War was over and the world had seen what had happened to Jews and other groups in the Nazi concentration camps, to Japanese prisoners of war, and to the people of Hiroshima and Nagasaki, the United Nations produced the Universal Declaration of

Human Rights. This sets out the basic rights which all the member countries believe are essential for every human being. There are 30 'articles' altogether, including:

Article 1: 'All human beings are born free and equal in dignity and rights.'
This means that all people have the same human rights as everyone else in the world, because you are a human being. These rights cannot be taken away from anyone. Every individual, no matter who they are or where they live, should be treated with dignity.

Article 2: 'Everyone is entitled to all the rights and freedoms set forth in this Declaration, without distinction of any kind.'
This means that people should not suffer discrimination, or be deprived of any of their rights, because of their race, colour, sex, language, religion or political opinions. It should not matter where they come from, or what their beliefs are, or how much money or power they have; the same rights apply to everyone.

Article 3: 'Everyone has the right to life, liberty and security of person.'
We all have the right to live in freedom and safety. No one should be killed, or kept in prison without good reasons.

Article 5: 'No one shall be subjected to torture or to cruel, inhuman or degrading treatment or punishment.'
Torture is never acceptable, in any circumstances, and when people have to be punished, it should be in a way that respects their dignity as human beings. This applies in police stations and prisons, in peacetime and in times of war.

Article 9: 'No one shall be subjected to arbitrary arrest, detention or exile.'
People may not be arrested or held in a police station or prison without good reason. Other people do not have the right to keep someone out of his or her own country. If people are detained, they have the right to challenge the detention in a court of law.

Article 18: 'Everyone has the right to freedom of thought, conscience and religion.'
People have the right to hold views on any issue that they like. They also have the right to believe in any religion – or none at all. They have the right to change their religion if they want to, and to practise and teach their religion or beliefs. No one should be able to punish them or treat them badly because of their beliefs.

These articles, and many others, have been agreed by the member countries of the United Nations, and are supported by all of the Christian Churches. If people believe that they have been treated in a way that is against this declaration, they can have their cases heard in international courts of appeal.

Although these guidelines exist, there are still many countries in the world where basic human rights are not recognised. People who disagree with the government are 'disappeared'; they are taken away by the police and put in prison or killed, but their families are never told where they are and the government denies knowing anything about it. People who voice opinions which disagree with government policy are tortured or executed. People with power and money are allowed to carry on with criminal activities, while the poor and uneducated are not given fair trials at all. Some people are held as 'prisoners of conscience'; they are locked up because of their religious or political beliefs, and sometimes just because of their colour or language.

Christians believe that all people have human rights, because they are all created by God in his image and loved by God as individuals. It is the duty of Christians to show the love of God by caring for the poor and weak, and by speaking out against injustice. Some Christians, because of their beliefs, are in favour of Liberation Theology. Some support organisations such as Amnesty International, which campaigns for human rights.

LIBERATION THEOLOGY

Many people are fortunate enough to live in countries where it is acceptable to protest against things that they disagree with. For example, in the UK, people are able to use their votes to show which government policies they agree with and which they oppose. They can stage demonstrations in the street to publicise a point of view. If they think that laws are wrong, they can write to the government or talk to their MPs about it. If they believe that the police have treated them unfairly, they can make a complaint about it. However, in some countries, this does not happen. The government will not accept any disagreement, and people who argue against it are imprisoned or executed, often without a fair trial. People who are the victims of injustice cannot say so without putting themselves at risk.

Liberation theology is a way of thinking that some Christians support, which argues that Christians should unite with the poor and the oppressed, and speak out against unjust governments and abuses of human rights. Followers of liberation theology believe that being kind to people who are poor or oppressed is not enough; the whole system should be challenged and changed so that they are not poor and oppressed any more.

Liberation theology has been particularly popular in Latin America, where the wealth of countries such as El Salvador and Chile has been owned by a small minority, while the rest of the people live in poverty. Most of the population of Latin America is Roman Catholic, and many Catholic priests have become involved in Liberation Theology, joining with the poor to try and make a fairer system for everyone. Many have put themselves in great danger, and have been imprisoned, tortured and even killed because of their beliefs.

Some, but not all, followers of Liberation Theology believe that human rights are so important that they must be fought for. If this cannot be done peacefully, then it has to involve the use of weapons so that the weak are defended.

Camilo Torres was a Roman Catholic priest who became involved in using violence on behalf of the poor. He lived in Colombia, and was appalled at the corruption of the government, which left the poor without proper food and shelter. People who stood up to the government 'disappeared', and the police made frequent raids on the homes of people who were believed to have anti-government opinions. Men, women and children were 'executed' without trial, and the whole population was living in terror. Camilo Torres' belief was that Christians have a duty to fight against unjust governments, and he joined Colombia's National Liberation Army; the first guerrilla movement to have Christians amongst its members. He called on all Christians to join in the

Oscar Romero, a Catholic priest, who was shot dead while celebrating mass, because of his support for the poor of El Salvador

FOR DISCUSSION

Make a list of arguments for, and arguments against, the use of violence by Christians who want to fight against injustice.

fight against oppression, saying 'Revolution is not only permitted for Christians, but obligatory'; it is something Christians must do. Camilo Torres was killed in action in 1966.

Oscar Romero was a Roman Catholic archbishop, who lived in El Salvador. Like Camilo Torres, he believed that Christians have a duty to defend the weak and make a stand against injustice. He spoke in his sermons about the rights of the poor, and openly criticised El Salvador's government. In 1980, while he was celebrating Mass, armed men burst into the cathedral and shot him dead in front of the altar. Other people, too, were killed for having listened to him. In spite of the dangers, there are many Christians who continue to believe that Liberation Theology is right.

Amnesty International is not a Christian organisation, but Christians might choose to support it

AMNESTY INTERNATIONAL

Amnesty International began in 1961, when a British lawyer called Peter Benenson read an article in a newspaper about two Portuguese students who had been sentenced to seven years' imprisonment for raising their glasses in a toast to freedom in a Lisbon bar. He believed that this sort of injustice should not be allowed to happen, and that if people got together and protested against it, governments would not be able to get away with this kind of bullying and intimidation.

Amnesty International describes itself as an organisation whose members are dedicated:

- to freeing prisoners of conscience
- to gaining fair trial for political prisoners
- to ending torture, political killings and 'disappearances'
- to abolishing the death penalty throughout the world.

When Amnesty International becomes aware of allegations of human rights abuses, it finds out the facts and then begins a campaign of letter-writing, publicity and protest to make people aware of what is going on. Its members argue that countries that use torture, or imprison people without fair trials, or use the death penalty, often try to do this in secret. If their behaviour is exposed to the rest of the world, they might be embarrassed enough to stop.

For example, if someone is kept in prison without a fair trial, and is tortured, and no one knows about it, then the police will continue to behave in this way. However, if an organisation like Amnesty International finds out about the prisoner, and lots of its members write to the government of the country about the prisoner, and they send the prisoner hundreds of letters and cards of support, then the government might think twice about its behaviour. It will realise that people are aware of what is going on, and might stop the torture and release the prisoner.

I was being kept naked in an underground cell. When the first 200 letters came, the guards gave me back my clothes. The next 200 letters came and the prison officers came to see me. When the next pile of letters arrived, the director got in touch with his superior. The letters kept coming, 3,000 of them, and the President called me to his office. He showed me an enormous box of letters he had received, and said: How is it that a trade union leader like you has so many friends all over the world?

(Union leader in the Dominican Republic, campaigned for by Amnesty International)

Amnesty International believes that it is very important to find out accurate information about a case before it begins its campaigns. It has a research department, which collects information from as many sources as it can: newspapers, broadcasts, reports from lawyers, as well as letters from the prisoners and their families. It also sends people to attend trials and to meet prisoners and government officials. Once the facts are known, it tries to publicise them as widely as possible, and it organises its members to begin letter-writing and campaigning.

Amnesty International aims to provide practical help to the people whose cases it takes up. It helps to ensure better treatment for them, and tries to persuade governments to allow doctors to visit prisoners if they have been tortured. In some cases, money is raised for food and clothing, and help is given when the prisoners have been released.

Amnesty International campaigns against abuses of human rights, such as torture and the death penalty

TORTURE

STAMP OUT TORTURE

DON'T LET THEM GET AWAY WITH IT

JOIN **AMNESTY INTERNATIONAL'S** CAMPAIGN TO STAMP OUT TORTURE

Amnesty International, 99-119 Rosebery Avenue, London, EC1R 4RE http://www.amnesty.org.uk CAMPAIGN HOTLINE: **020 7417 6385**

ICT FOR RESEARCH

Visit the web-site of Amnesty International:

www.amnesty.org.uk

Find out more about the campaigns, and the ways in which Amnesty International is supported by its local branches.

As well as working on behalf of individuals, Amnesty International tries to change laws and policies so that people's basic human rights are better protected. It was involved in campaigning for an international ban on the use of torture, and for the abolition of the death penalty in the UK and other countries. It also worked for the setting up of an international court of justice, which 120 nations agreed to set up in 1998, so that people responsible for human rights abuses can be brought to trial without the protection of corrupt governments.

Amnesty International is against capital punishment (the death penalty) in all cases. Its research department shows that capital punishment has never reduced crime rates more effectively than other punishments, and its members believe that it goes against the Universal Declaration of Human Rights and is the worst form of torture. Amnesty International takes action to prevent condemned prisoners from being executed, and it campaigns to persuade governments to abolish the death penalty in law.

The contribution of Amnesty International to human rights has been recognised internationally. Amnesty International was awarded the Nobel Peace Prize in 1977, and the United Nations Human Rights Prize in 1978.

CHRISTIANS AND AMNESTY INTERNATIONAL

Although Amnesty International is not a Christian organisation, many Christians support it because it is a way of putting Christian beliefs into practice. Joining together with other people gives individuals the power to do something about human rights abuses. Christians might feel that joining Amnesty International is a good way of demonstrating their beliefs about the value of every human life, and a good way of putting the principle of agape into practice.

PRACTICE EXAMINATION QUESTIONS

1 (a) **Describe Biblical teaching which might be used to support pacifism. (8 marks)**

Notice that here, you are asked for Biblical teaching, so you should confine your answer to material that is from the Bible. You are asked to present teachings which might be used to support pacifism, but you are not asked to give another point of view, so you can concentrate only on the teachings about peace.

(b) **Explain why some Christians might choose to fight for their countries in times of war. (7 marks)**

You could explain Christian teaching about defence of the weak, and give some examples of Church teaching, such as the Just War theory. Try to think of more than one reason.

(c) **'The Bible was written too long ago to have anything useful to say about wars today.' Do you agree? Give reasons to support your answer, and show that you have thought about different points of view. You must refer to Christianity in your answer. (5 marks)**

You could show that you know that the nature of warfare has changed a lot since the Bible was written, but you should concentrate your answer on presenting arguments rather than describing facts. Remember to include a Christian point of view – you might think of using some of the information from Chapter 1 (Background) on the importance of the Bible for Christians.

2 (a) **Describe Christian teaching about human rights. (8 marks)**

Remember to show that you know that the International Declaration of Human Rights is not Christian, although the Churches all support it. Try to give specifically Christian teachings, such as the idea of the sanctity of life.

(b) **Explain why Christians might choose to support the work of an organisation which helps the victims of human rights abuses. (7 marks)**

Remember that Amnesty International is not a Christian organisation, but Christians might support it. You can include some description of what the organisation does, but you should concentrate on how this fits in with Christian beliefs.

(c) **'Sometimes using violence is the best way to fight against injustice.' Do you agree? Give reasons to support your answer, and show that you have thought about different points of view. You must refer to Christianity in your answer. (5 marks)**

Remember to give more than one point of view here, including a Christian response. You could give some examples of people who have felt that violence, or non-violence, is the best choice.

CHRISTIAN RESPONSIBILITY FOR THE PLANET

Christian teaching relating to the problems facing the planet: the world as the creation of God, the concept of stewardship, environmental issues and Christian responses to them.

BIBLICAL TEACHING – THE WORLD AS THE CREATION OF GOD

When you open a book, and read the first sentence, it often gives you some idea of the sort of book you are about to read; it sets the scene. The Bible is no exception. The very first words of the Bible are probably some of the most famous:

> *In the beginning God created the heavens and the earth.* (Genesis 1: 1)

The Bible teaches that the planet was created by God, and belongs to God

The scene is set: God was present at the very beginning of the world, and the world is his creation.

In the creation story, God makes all the different components of the earth and of the skies, and puts them into place. As each part of the creation is completed, the Bible says: 'And God saw that it was good'. This implies that, at the start, there was nothing wrong with the planet, and it all worked very well.

Although the Bible appears to give several different opinions on some subjects, it is completely consistent in the view that the world belongs to God, as his creation. For example, many of the Psalms praise God for the creation of the world:

> *For the LORD is the great God, the great King above all gods. In his hand are the depths of the earth, and the mountain peaks belong to him. The sea is his, for he made it, and his hands formed the dry land. Come, let us bow down in worship, let us kneel before the LORD our Maker.*
>
> (Psalm 95: 3–6)

> *The earth is the LORD's, and everything in it, the world, and all who live in it; for he founded it upon the seas and established it upon the waters.*
>
> (Psalm 24: 1–2)

Psalm 19 begins by drawing attention to the heavens, or the skies, and explains that although they cannot speak, they reveal the glory of God more completely than any human language:

> *The heavens declare the glory of God; the skies proclaim the work of his hands. Day after day they pour forth speech; night after night they display knowledge. There is no speech or language where their voice is not heard. Their voice goes out into all the earth, their words to the ends of the world.*
>
> (Psalm 19: 1–4)

The Psalm moves on to talk about the laws of God, which are also seen as part of creation. The laws of astronomy were made by God, and God also made laws about the ways in which people should behave. This Psalm, therefore, teaches that God is in control of the whole universe, and that people have a duty to keep to God's laws, which are as perfect as the movement of the planets.

The New Testament does not give the same emphasis to the concept of the world as the creation of God, but there are passages which show the same underlying belief that God created and cares for every living thing:

> *Look at the birds of the air; they do not sow or reap or store away in barns, and yet your heavenly Father feeds them. Are you not much more valuable than they? ... See how the lilies of the field grow. They do not labour or spin. Yet I tell you that not even Solomon in all his splendour was dressed like one of these.*
>
> (Matthew 6: 26–29)

THE CONCEPT OF STEWARDSHIP

The very first law given to humanity, as soon as the first human was created in the image of God, was that they should be 'stewards' of the earth. A steward is someone who acts in a care-taking role; for example, a steward at a music festival might show people where to park their cars, help to re-unite lost children with their parents, deal with First Aid and encourage people to behave in a safe and orderly way. A 'shop steward' is a member of a Trade Union, who represents the workers whenever there is a disagreement with the management, looking after the workers' interests and making sure that they are treated in a fair and legal manner. So being a steward involves working on behalf of the owner or organiser, serving others, representing the interests of the most vulnerable, making sure that everything stays as it should be and does not get out of hand, and keeping things safe.

When humans are made as stewards of the earth, they are given this same care-taking role:

Then God said, 'Let us make man in our image, in our likeness, and let them rule over the fish of the sea and the birds of the air, over the livestock, over all the earth, and over all the creatures that move along the ground.' So God created man in his own image, in the image of God he created him; male and female he created them. God blessed them and said to them, 'Be fruitful and increase in number; fill the earth and subdue it. Rule over the fish of the sea and the birds of the air and over every living creature that moves on the ground.'

Then God said, 'I give you every seed-bearing plant on the face of the whole earth and every tree that has fruit with seed in it. They will be yours for food. And to all the beasts of the earth and the birds of the air and all the creatures that move on the ground – everything that has the breath of life in it – I give every green plant for food.' And it was so.

God saw all that he had made, and it was very good.

(Genesis 1: 26–31)

Christians believe that the beauty of the world reveals something of the nature of God

People are in charge of all the living things that have been made on the earth – but they do not own them. They have to look after God's belongings.

In another of the Psalms, the writer expresses a sense of wonder when looking at the night sky, and thinks about the enormous privilege and responsibility stewardship is:

O LORD, our Lord, how majestic is your name in all the earth!

You have set your glory above the heavens …

When I consider your heavens, the work of your fingers, the moon and the stars, which you have set in place, what is man that you are mindful of him, the son of man that you care for him?

You made him a little lower than the heavenly beings and crowned him with glory and honour.

You made him ruler over the works of your hands; you put everything under his feet.

(Psalm 8: 1, 3–6)

Some of the rules of the Old Testament are about good stewardship; for example, rules are given about harvesting. In Old Testament times, 'gleaning' was a common practice. After a field had been harvested, any grain which had fallen on the ground or which had been missed by the harvesters was left for the poor, who would be allowed to go and collect it for their own use. The book of Ruth gives an example of this – the widowed Ruth, who was caring for her mother-in-law Naomi in a time of famine, went to glean in Bethlehem after the barley harvest, and it was here that she met her second husband, Boaz. Boaz is shown as being a good man, because he allowed the gleaners onto his land.

'Gleaning' was a way in which poor people could find food, by gathering the grain the harvesters had left behind

> *When you are harvesting in your field and you overlook a sheaf, do not go back and get it. Leave it for the alien, the fatherless and the widow, so that the LORD your God may bless you in all the work of your hands. When you beat the olives from your trees, do not go over the branches a second time. Leave what remains for the alien, the fatherless and the widow. When you harvest the grapes in your vineyard, do not go over the vines again. Leave what remains for the alien, the fatherless and the widow. Remember that you were slaves in Egypt. That is why I command you to do this.*
>
> (Deuteronomy 24: 19–22)

The law reminds people not to insist on taking every last scrap for themselves; they should make sure that they leave something behind for the people who will come after them.

PROBLEMS FACING THE PLANET

All of our water, food, medicines and fuel come from the world's natural resources. However, human population has grown rapidly, and so has our consumption of these resources, many of which are 'non-renewable', which means that once they have been used, they cannot be replaced.

THE OZONE LAYER

The ozone layer surrounds the earth, forming a barrier of oxygen that filters out ultra-violet rays from the sun. However, many of the ozone molecules have been destroyed by human use of chlorofluorocarbons (CFCs) in aerosols and refrigerators. Although the use of CFCs has been drastically reduced since scientists made governments aware of the problem, a lot of damage has already been done. There are large holes in the ozone layer, and the dangerous ultra-violet rays are affecting health, causing eye cataracts and skin cancers. Children in Australia are no longer allowed to play outside unless they wear large shady hats, because the hole in the ozone layer over Australia means that even in primary school, boys and girls have been developing melanomas (skin cancer).

In Australia, children are encouraged to wear shady hats and to keep covered up, because the hole in the ozone layer increases the risk of skin cancer

Rainforest wildlife is seriously at risk from deforestation

GLOBAL WARMING

One of the biggest problems facing the world today is climate change, often known as 'global warming'. Scientists have been warning governments that this is a very real and serious problem. The earth is surrounded by a thin layer of gases, which are carefully balanced and which maintain the different climates that the world needs in order to sustain the different life forms within it. However, the balance of these gases is being destroyed, by a build-up of carbon dioxide, and the earth is no longer being kept at the right temperature but is becoming gradually warmer.

The extra carbon dioxide is being produced because of the destruction of the rainforests (see 'deforestation'), by the millions of cars used every day, and because of the ways in which industrialised countries produce waste gases during manufacturing processes. In particular, the burning of fossil fuels such as gas, coal and oil create an excess amount of carbon dioxide. Scientists point out that we are dangerously close to the 'safe' limit for global warming; if we allow the earth's temperature to rise much further, polar ice-caps will melt and the sea levels will rise dramatically, causing frequent storms and hurricanes, massive flooding and loss of life.

DEFORESTATION

Half of the world's rainforests have been destroyed since the Second World War. 'Deforestation' means clearing away forests permanently, so that the wood can be sold by timber companies and the land can be put to other uses, such as farming, mining or building. The rainforests only cover about 6% of the total surface of the earth, but they contain more than 50% of its species – plants, some of which provide the only natural source of important medicines, insects which play an important role in the world's eco-systems, and many beautiful animals.

Every week, an area of rainforest the size of the UK is cleared. Many different species have become extinct, because their natural habitat has been destroyed, and the effects of this destruction are still unfolding. We do not yet know how deforestation will affect the world in the long-term.

Domestic rubbish and industrial waste cause pollution

POLLUTION

Pollution affects the world in many different ways. Industrialised countries produce huge amounts of waste: poisonous gases, which cause respiratory problems and acid rain; nuclear waste, which contaminates the seas and causes cancers and birth defects; and other toxic waste in the form of chemicals which are very difficult to dispose of safely. Each household in the UK produces more than a tonne of domestic rubbish each year, and another tonne of toxic waste per person is produced by industries. Farmers use chemical pesticides to make their land more productive, and these are washed into rivers by rain, poisoning the fish, birds and insects, and affecting drinking water.

ENVIRONMENTAL DAMAGE TO THE SEAS

Damage to the seas is particularly important, because so much of the surface of the earth is covered by water. It is also one of the most difficult problems to control, because the seas do not technically 'belong' to any particular country, and so there is nothing to ensure that anyone takes responsibility for protecting them. The seas are used as a convenient place for dumping waste, such as toxic waste, nuclear waste and raw sewage. Over-fishing and habitat loss has pushed the numbers of fish to their lowest level ever; and fish are a vital food for many of the world's poorest countries, where they are often a major source of protein.

THE INVOLVEMENT OF THE CHRISTIAN CHURCHES

Some people believe that the Christian Churches should take some of the blame for environmental problems. Christianity has given people the impression that it is right that they should rule over other species and put themselves first, and this could have given rise to arrogant attitudes, where humans believe that it is acceptable for them to kill other animals for food, for fur or even just for fun. The idea of humanity having 'dominion' over the world has led people to believe that they are in charge, that they are more important than the rest of the world, and that they can use up whatever they want in the world as long as it suits their needs. Christianity teaches that humans are set apart from other animals, because they are made in the image of God. Other people might argue against this, and say that although humans are the most intelligent species, this does not give them the right to kill or to make other animals suffer.

In recent years, the Churches have become much more aware of damage to the environment, and are conscious that people have failed to be responsible stewards.

There have been many discussion groups and conferences, aiming to produce positive ways in which the Churches can act with other people in an effort to reduce damage to the environment.

The **Church of England**, for example, in 1992, agreed to take all possible steps to minimise pollution and to use the world's energy resources carefully. It agreed to work towards reducing the damage to plants and animals, and also to take positive steps towards population control.

The **Roman Catholic Church** teaches that people have a responsibility to think about the amount we consume, and that we should plan for the welfare of future generations, as well as considering the impact that the behaviour of richer countries has on the developing nations.

All of the Churches agree that it is an important part of a Christian's duty to look after the planet, and to be responsible stewards. They teach that the Christian principle of agape (love) extends to future generations, as well as our own.

CHRISTIAN RESPONSES TO ENVIRONMENTAL ISSUES

Christians might put their faith into action in a variety of ways:

- They could use their votes in favour of candidates who show concern for environmental issues.
- They could pray about the problems of the environment.
- They could try to cut down on the amount they waste at home, by choosing products with the minimum packaging, and recycling wherever possible, for example using bottle banks and making garden compost.
- They could make an effort to use less fuel in the home, by buying energy-efficient household appliances, insulating their homes properly to use less heating, and investigating the use of solar power.
- They could organise car-sharing, or walk or cycle to work, to reduce the number of cars on the road and the energy consumption and pollution that result from too much traffic.
- They could become involved in protests about environmental issues, by writing to MPs or taking part in marches and demonstrations.
- They could join an organisation which works to promote conservation.

ICT FOR RESEARCH

Visit the Church of England web-site on:

www.cofe.anglican.org/

Go to the section called 'The Church of England's view on ...' and read the statements that have been made on the environment and animal welfare.

FOR DISCUSSION

Why do you think that so many people do not take environmental issues very seriously?

ICT FOR RESEARCH

Visit the Christian ecology web-site:

www.christian-ecology.org.uk/

Find out more about how care for the environment relates to Christian beliefs.

Scientists are working to develop new ways of creating energy without wasting natural resources

ORGANISATIONS WHICH CHRISTIANS MIGHT CHOOSE TO SUPPORT

There are many different organisations in existence which work to help the environment. Three of the most famous are Greenpeace, the Worldwide Fund for Nature, and Friends of the Earth. All of them are involved in campaigns and protests to encourage governments to change their policies and reduce waste and damage. For example, as part of Greenpeace's campaign to protect the ozone layer, Greenpeace developed Greenfreeze technology, which is a cooling system that is safe both for the ozone layer and the climate. Greenpeace wants this solution to be applied throughout the world to replace HFC refrigeration. Friends of the Earth is one of the leading environmental pressure groups in the UK, and is made up of many small local groups. It uses donations to fund research projects, and puts pressure on the government to support renewable energy sources such as wind turbines, sea power and solar power.

The Worldwide Fund for Nature has a Living Planet campaign, which aims to draw attention to the fact that 30% of the world's plants and animals have been lost over the last three generations, and tries to make people aware of the urgency of the problem. It encourages individuals, companies and governments to adopt 'green' policies, and has four main areas of campaign: Climate Change, Endangered Seas, Forests for Life and Living Waters.

None of these organisations has its basis in Christianity, but Christians might choose to support them or one of the many other campaigns, as a way of putting into practice their beliefs about stewardship and concern for others, including future generations.

ICT FOR RESEARCH

Visit one or more of the following web-sites to find out more about the work of organisations which aim to conserve the environment.
Friends of the Earth:
www.foe.co.uk/
Greenpeace:
www.greenpeace.org/
WWF: www.panda.org/

IN YOUR NOTES

Summarise the work of the organisation you have chosen, and give some examples of projects with which it is involved.

PRACTICE EXAMINATION QUESTION

1 (a) Describe Christian teaching about steward-ship. (8 marks)

Remember to use Biblical examples, as well as the teaching of the Churches. You do not have to remember long passages of the Bible by heart; short phrases such as 'the image of God' and 'have dominion' are quite acceptable as long as you show you understand what they mean.

(b) Explain how a Christian might show concern for the world's environmental problems. (7 marks)

Try to give a range of different examples, rather than concentrating on just one.

(c) 'The environment is a problem for governments, not individuals.'

Do you agree? Give reasons to support your answer, and show that you have thought about different points of view. You must refer to Christianity in your answer. (5 marks)

Remember that you need to show you have thought about more than one side to the argument; and you need to include Christian views in your discussion.

CHRISTIAN RESPONSIBILITY TOWARDS DISADVANTAGED PEOPLE

Christian attitudes towards the poor and the weak. Biblical teaching, the responses of the Churches to poverty, and the work of at least one explicitly Christian aid organisation, e.g. Christian Aid, CAFOD or Tearfund.

WORLD POVERTY: THE NORTH–SOUTH DIVIDE

The world today is very sharply divided between the rich and the poor. This division is often known as the North–South divide, because most of the rich countries are north of the Equator: the USA, Western European countries including the UK, and Japan, for example. These are often known as the Developed World, or sometimes the First World. Only a quarter of the world's population lives in the Developed World, but these countries use up more than three-quarters of the world's resources (food, fuel etc) every year. There is enough food in the world for everyone to have more than three thousand calories a day, if equal shares were available for everyone. However, because people in the rich North want to have so much, the people in the South have to go without.

Australia and New Zealand are also rich countries, but most of the other countries south of the Equator are very poor, including South America, Africa, and India. These are known as the Developing World or the Third World, where three-quarters of the world's population have only a fifth of the world's resources to share between them.

In the Developed World, most people expect to live until they are at least 70. They are educated until they are about 16, and often for longer. Most people choose how many children to have, and expect them to survive to adulthood. Children of 12, at the turn of the millennium, sometimes receive as much as £10 a week in pocket money. People in the Developed World have problems with heart disease and obesity (being overweight), but they also have easy access to health care. They own nearly all of the world's manufacturing industries, and they control world banks, deciding how much different currencies are worth and making the rules about borrowing and repaying money.

In contrast, in the Developing World, life expectancy is 50 years or below, and in some countries, more than half of the population is aged under 14, which means that the country as a whole consumes more than it is able to produce. One child in seven dies before reaching the age of 5. Most of the people in the Developing World have an income of less than £1.25 a week. People suffer from hunger and from malnutrition, and 20 million people die every year because of inadequate food. Safe clean water is rarely available. Health care is scarce and often too expensive for ordinary people, and there are high levels of illiteracy, particularly amongst women. The countries of the Developing World have very little power, and are trapped by owing large amounts to richer countries; paying off these debts makes the rich even richer and the poor even poorer.

SOME STATISTICS

For every 1000 people in Canada, there are 221 doctors. For every 1000 people in Haiti, there are 16.

A woman in the UK can expect to live for an average of 79.4 years. In Bangladesh, she can expect to reach 57.

The Developed World has access to 94% of the world's health care. So 6% is left for the other three quarters of the world's population.

(Statistics supplied by CAFOD, 2000)

In rich countries, people can buy whatever they need. Food, housing and clean water are taken for granted

Mali, in western Africa, uses only eight litres of water for each person each day. In the UK, this amount of water is used every time someone flushes a toilet.

The amount of money that people in Europe spend on ice cream each year would be enough to cover the cost of providing clean water to all the people in developing countries.

(Statistics supplied by Tearfund, 2000)

World poverty is an enormous problem. There are many contributing factors, but one fact is inescapable: poverty exists because people in the Developed World are unwilling to change the way they live. Although we might think that our country gives a generous amount to the poor in overseas aid, in fact the poor countries have been giving far more to rich countries than they receive in return, because of the ways in which world debt and interest rates have been organised.

THE BRANDT REPORT

In 1980, Willy Brandt, the former Chancellor of West Germany, was the chairman of a commission which was set up to look into the issue of world poverty. Reports were produced describing the extent of the problem, the differences between the rich and poor, and the reasons for these differences. The findings were put into a document called the Brandt Report.

Conditions are unlikely to change for people in the Developing World unless the richer countries are prepared to change

This was very important, because before the Brandt Report was published, many people still believed that the way to deal with extreme poverty was to send food or money in times of crisis. The Brandt Report showed the world that this was not enough, and that nothing would change unless much more long-term action was taken. The causes of poverty had to be explored and tackled, and this involved making changes in the Developed World as well as the Developing World.

Unfortunately, although the Brandt Report highlighted the seriousness of the problem and set out the things that needed to be done, things have got worse rather than better.

THE CAUSES OF POVERTY

POPULATION

Many people believe that one of the main reasons why poorer countries stay poor is that they have too many children. The population of the world is growing rapidly, particularly in the developing countries. Some people say that the poor countries would be able to feed themselves if they had smaller families. However, the situation is not as simple as this.

People in poor countries need to have large families in order to survive. They cannot grow their crops without help, but they are too poor to employ staff, so they have children who can provide them with extra labour. There is no state pension or any other kind of state care for the elderly, so children are needed so that they can look after their parents when they become too frail to be able to look after themselves. Many children die in infancy, so families need to have more than one or two to make sure that there are enough survivors. In rich countries, people do not need to have many children, and so their families are smaller; but they still consume most of the world's food.

DISASTERS

Disasters seem to occur on a regular basis in the Developing World. It is difficult to open a newspaper or watch the television news without looking at a flood in Bangladesh, or a drought in Sudan, and sometimes we might feel that we see these stories so often that they are not even particularly interesting. However, disasters causing floods, disease and famine have a huge impact on developing countries. Because the people are poor, they cannot afford to live in places which are safer – those are already taken by people who have more money. Because they are poor,

A flood in Bangladesh leaves many people with nothing

their homes are flimsy and easily destroyed. Because the country is poor, it does not have a supply of extra food and medicines when disasters happen. In rich countries such as Japan, the USA and Australia, the houses are built to withstand earthquakes and cyclones, and communication is good enough for people to have plenty of warning if a disaster is about to happen. They will have somewhere else to go, and will have stored food and emergency supplies, so that a 'disaster' is much less traumatic.

CONFLICT

One of the causes of poverty is war – either war against another country, or war within a country (civil war) where one group of people is fighting another. When countries experience armed conflict, they have to spend money on weapons, when the money could have been used for education, health or agriculture. War destroys valuable services such as schools, bridges and hospitals. Landmines make areas unsuitable to farm, and war involves people in fighting when they could have been planting and harvesting crops. Transport is much more difficult, making it hard for food supplies to be shared out to the people who need them. People lose their homes if they are destroyed, or they leave an area because it is too dangerous, and they become refugees.

DEBT AND FAIR TRADE

In many developing countries, such as Haiti, Honduras and Zambia, debt is a major problem. These countries have had to take out loans from the International Monetary Fund (IMF) in order to help their economies to survive. The debts have to be paid with interest, and the countries often end up owing far more than they can afford to pay back. The IMF then imposes Structural Adjustment Programmes, which force the developing countries to cut down on their spending on areas such as health care and education, so that they can make the debt repayments.

The rich Developed World in the North buys goods such as sugar, cotton and coffee from the poor South, and the South uses the money to help build economies and to pay off money that was borrowed from rich countries in order to survive. However, the poor countries receive lower and lower prices for the goods they export. The rich people in the North want to be able to buy their groceries cheaply, and the major supermarket chains have 'price wars' to see which can attract the most customers. The buyers in the North are only prepared to offer the growers in the South very little money. At the same time, the Developing World has to pay higher and higher prices for the goods it needs to import, such as farm machinery. It has to grow more crops to sell to the North, using land that could have been used to feed its own population. In Kenya, for example,

IN YOUR NOTES

(a) Why is the Developing World in so much debt?

(b) What effect does this have on people in poverty?

(c) Explain the main causes of poverty in the Developing World.

women reported having to grow tobacco right up to the doors of their houses, with no land left for the family's vegetables; and they still did not earn enough money for adequate food. The Developing World cannot keep up with the demands made by the North, and more money has to be borrowed, increasing the debt and continuing the vicious cycle. Africa's interest payments on its debts cost four times as much as it spends on health care. In Zambia, between 1990 and 1993, debt repayments cost 34 times as much as the country was able to spend on primary school education – education spending fell by more than 80%.

A project called **Jubilee 2000** was set up to try and put pressure on governments to cancel world debt and allow the poorest countries to use their money to supply basic needs, rather than having to spend it on repayments. The Church called the year 2000 a Jubilee year, because of its commemoration of two thousand years of Christianity. In the Bible, a rule is made that in the Year of Jubilee, debts are to be cancelled and slaves are to be freed:

> He and his children are to be released in the Year of Jubilee. (Leviticus 25: 54)

Many different Christians from around the world joined together to protest against world debt and to campaign for change.

Many workers in the Developing World have to put up with conditions that are illegal in the UK. They are expected to work between 12 and 14 hours a day, without overtime payment, for an average wage of just 40p per day, or £17 per week, which does not meet basic family needs and gives children little chance of secondary education. Workers can be sacked without notice and with no redundancy payment. Sometimes the chemicals used in agriculture affect their health. The big companies often control all aspects of local life, including schools, medical care and water supplies, so that it is impossible for the workers to protest without losing everything.

The Fairtrade Mark is an independent consumer label first launched in March 1994. It highlights products which are guaranteed to give better prices to farmers, or decent wages and reasonable working conditions to producers in the Developing World. The Fairtrade Mark can be found on coffee, tea, cocoa, chocolate and honey, in supermarkets and health food or fair trade shops such as Oxfam.

'Then they also will answer, "Lord, when was it that we saw you hungry or thirsty or a stranger or naked or sick or in prison, and did not take care of you?"' (Matthew 25: 44)

The Fairtrade Mark on a product means that it has been produced in a way that does not exploit the workers

FOR DISCUSSION

Do you think that the Developed World could do something about world debt? If so, what could it do?

In order to qualify for a Fairtrade Mark, suppliers have to meet the following conditions:

- They have to pay what is, for the area, a fair wage.
- They have to provide equal employment opportunities, and show concern for the most disadvantaged.
- They must use environmentally friendly methods of production.
- They must provide healthy and safe working conditions.

Fairtrade bananas can now be found in many major supermarket chains. Bananas have overtaken apples as the world's most popular fruit, and they are the third best-selling product in supermarkets after petrol and National Lottery tickets. Because bananas are so important to the supermarkets, the supermarket owners want to keep the price low. They have been buying bananas from companies which are cheap because they save money by giving appallingly low wages to their workers, and they save by not bothering to give them safety equipment, such as masks to protect them from dangerous chemical gases. Now that Fairtrade bananas have been introduced, customers in the UK can choose to buy bananas from small family farms or estates which pay their workers in the Developing World more than the minimum wage and use environmentally friendly methods of growing.

Another example of ethical shopping in action is the Rugmark. The Rugmark is a label put onto hand-crafted oriental rugs, to show that they have been produced without the labour of little children. In the Developing World, many children as young as 6 or 7 spend long hours sitting in factories knotting rugs to sell to countries in the North. This affects their health – they do not get enough fresh air and exercise, and their eyesight is damaged, often permanently. They also miss out on education, and drastically reduce their chances of ever having a better standard of living in the future.

EDUCATION AND CHILD LABOUR

In the poorest countries, fewer than half of all adults can read or write, and most children never have the chance to go to secondary school. Illiteracy is a particular problem for women; two-thirds of the people in the world who cannot read or write are female. If families can only afford to educate one or two of their children, they will choose the boys, because in traditional societies it is still the boys who grow up to become the heads of their families. Women produce much of the world's food, working in the fields, and then at the beginning and end of the day they also work at home – cooking, washing, cleaning and taking care of the children. Girls are often needed at home to help their mothers, while girls in the Developed World are still in infants' schools.

Child labour is a huge problem in the Developing World. According

Child labour is a great problem in Developing Countries. This child has little hope of an education

to figures from the International Labour Organisation, in 2000 more than 250 million children between the ages of 5 and 14 are working, often in dangerous conditions. Some work in factories, some in the fields, and others on the streets. Parents cannot afford to lose the small wages that the children provide, and so the children cannot go to school but are trapped in a cycle of poverty and illiteracy. UNICEF is one aid organisation that works to change the law, to make it illegal to employ children under the age of 14, and to encourage governments to provide families with a small amount of money to compensate for the loss of their children's earnings.

A lack of education makes it very difficult for people to change the way that they live. Employment opportunities for people who have no literacy skills are very limited. Being unable to read or write can be a great handicap in many ways, for example it makes receiving health education much more difficult.

Many people who work with aid agencies point out the need for education for the rich, as well as for the poor. The poor desperately need to be taught basic skills which will help them to read instructions on machinery or medicines, and to realise when they are being exploited. However, the rich also need to be educated about the impact their behaviour has on the developing countries. People in the North do not usually set out to buy goods which come from companies that cheat the

FOR DISCUSSION

Do you think that if you knew more about the Developing World, it would change the way that you live?

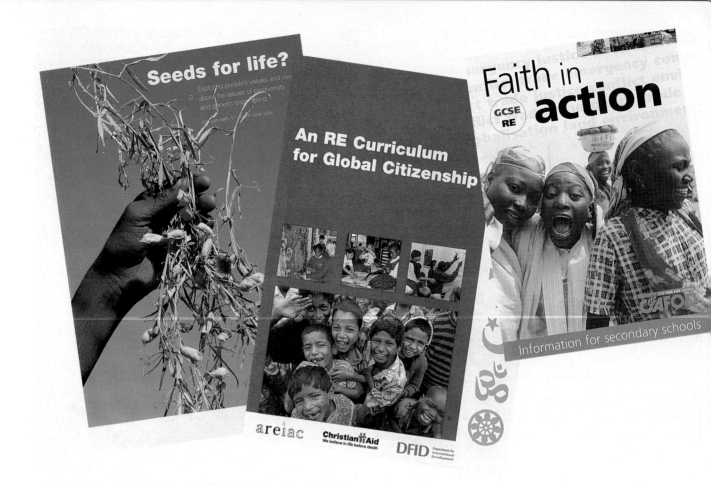

Education for people in rich countries is essential if things are going to change. Many aid agencies spend some of their income on education

poor, for example; they simply do not know what is going on. Many aid agencies spend some of their income providing information and education for rich countries, to raise awareness. They argue that a major change is needed in the attitude of the Developed World – people need to stop measuring success by the amount they consume and stop aiming towards extravagant, wasteful lifestyles.

POVERTY IN THE UK

Poverty is not just a problem for the Developing World, although its effects there are much more serious than they are in the UK. Although the scale of the problem is less in the UK, and very few people die of hunger, there is still a noticeable difference between the lifestyles of the rich and the poor. During the 1980s, the gap between rich and poor grew wider. The income of the lower half of the population fell, while the income of the richest 20% increased dramatically.

About one in three children in the UK lives in poverty – a total of 4½ million. Their families are unable to provide them with the basic things they need. Over a million children live in homes where both parents are unemployed

When there is a large gap between rich and poor, this leads to other kinds of inequality too. Children from lower income families are unlikely to do as well at school, because they often do not have a quiet place at home where they can study, and they might have to take on jobs such as working on a market stall to help out with money at home. They are more likely to live in conditions which make them ill. They are more likely to become involved with crime or drugs, because they have to live in areas where this is happening all around them. Of course, not all people from low income families do badly at school or commit crimes, but it is much more difficult for them to reach the same levels of achievement that are available to richer families.

The Salvation Army is an example of a Christian organisation that works to help people in the UK. It has branches all over the world, but it is especially famous for its work with the poor and the homeless in the UK. The government is the largest organisation in the UK that provides services for poor people, and The Salvation Army is the second largest. It provides shelters and hostels for homeless people, so that they have somewhere safe and clean where they can sleep at night. It runs a large 'Missing Persons' network, where people who have left home because they have felt unable to cope are able to get in touch with relatives. It provides care for the elderly, in sheltered accommodation and nursing homes, and runs over-60s clubs where lonely people can get together for tea and a chat. There are children's homes, and respite services to give the families of children with special needs an occasional break.

Salvationists believe that Christianity means nothing unless it is put into action. They believe that preaching the Gospel is very important for Christians, and that one of the best ways of telling people about Christian love is to go out and do it.

The Salvation Army works among people in need

ICT FOR RESEARCH

Visit the Salvation Army web-site:
www.salvationarmy.org.uk
Find out more about the ways in which The Salvation Army works with people in the UK. Read about the beliefs of members of The Salvation Army, and find out how the organisation began in Victorian times.

BIBLICAL TEACHING ABOUT CARE FOR THE POOR

In the Old Testament, there are plenty of occasions when the people are given laws by God which make it clear that they are to care for the poor and treat them with justice:

> *Do not ill-treat an alien or oppress him, for you were aliens in Egypt. Do not take advantage of a widow or an orphan ... If you lend money to one of my people among you who is needy, do not be like a money-lender; charge him no interest.* (Exodus 22: 21–22,25)
>
> *When you reap the harvest of your land, do not reap to the very edges of your field or gather the gleanings of your harvest. Leave them for the poor and the alien. I am the LORD your God.* (Leviticus 23: 22)
>
> *If one of your countrymen becomes poor and is unable to support himself among you, help him as you would an alien or a temporary resident, so that he can continue to live among you ... You must not lend him money at interest or sell him food at a profit.* (Leviticus 25: 35, 37)

These are just a few examples. Loving God involves keeping the commandments; the people were told time and time again that they should respond to God by caring for each other, and especially for those in need.

> *And he has given us this command: Whoever loves God must also love his brother.* (1 John 4: 21)

Amos was an Old Testament prophet who lived in the eighth century BCE. The role of a prophet is to pass messages from God to the people, and Amos, although he was only an ordinary sheep-farmer, took on this role with great eloquence and passion. The message that Amos was given to tell everyone was quite clear: the people had offended God and were going to be punished severely. Although the people had been performing all the proper religious rituals, God was not impressed, because when they were not taking part in worship, they were cheating the poor:

> *I hate, I despise your religious feasts; I cannot stand your assemblies ... Away with the noise of your songs! I will not listen to the music of your harps. But let justice roll on like a river, righteousness like a never-failing stream!* (Amos 5: 21, 23–24)

Amos described how the people had been so greedy that instead of thinking about God on the Sabbath, they had been wishing that it would soon be over, so that they could get back to making money. They had been cheating other people by fixing the scales in their shops so that customers were given less than they had paid for, and they had been treating the poor as if they were worth nothing more than a cheap pair of shoes:

> *Hear this, you who trample the needy and do away with the poor of the land, saying, 'When will the New Moon be over that we may sell grain, and the Sabbath be ended that we may market wheat?' – skimping the measure, boosting the price and cheating with dishonest scales, buying the poor with silver and the needy for a pair of sandals, selling even the sweepings with the wheat.* (Amos 8: 4–6)

Amos was not alone in expressing God's anger with people who did nothing to help the poor; the prophet Isaiah also told people about the need for showing love to people in need:

> *... and if you spend yourselves on behalf of the hungry and satisfy the needs of the oppressed, then your light will rise in the darkness, and your night will become like the noonday.* (Isaiah 58: 10)

In the New Testament, too, concern for the poor is given a very prominent place, particularly in Luke's Gospel. When Jesus began his ministry in Nazareth, he quoted a passage from the prophet Isaiah, as a way of stating what he intended to do:

> 'The spirit of the LORD is upon me, because he has anointed me to preach good news to the poor.
> He has sent me to proclaim freedom for the prisoners and recovery of sight for the blind,
> to release the oppressed,
> to proclaim the year of the LORD's favour.'
>
> (Luke 4: 18–19)

Many people in the time of Jesus believed that wealth was a sign of blessing, and that the rich should be respected because God had rewarded them. Jesus' teaching gave a very different message:

> Looking at his disciples, he said: 'Blessed are you who are poor, for yours is the kingdom of God. Blessed are you who hunger now, for you will be satisfied. Blessed are you who weep now, for you will laugh.
>
> (Luke 6: 20-21)

The poor were shown to have a special place with God. All of the gospel writers show that Jesus taught a message of love for others and concern for the weak, but Luke in particular stressed this.

Jesus taught, with his words and his actions, that love (agape) is not just a feeling; it has to be put into practice. It is wrong to live a comfortable life-style and enjoy luxuries when there are poor people around who need help. It is disobedient to the Two Greatest Commandments:

> Love the LORD your God with all your heart and with all your soul and with all your mind and with all your strength ... Love your neighbour as yourself.
>
> (Mark 12: 30–31)

Two parables in particular make the point that it is very wrong to do nothing for the poor. The parable of Dives and Lazarus in Luke's Gospel shows how Dives is condemned for ignoring the man who begs at his gate:

> There was a rich man who was dressed in purple and fine linen and lived in luxury every day. At his gate was laid a beggar named Lazarus, covered with sores and longing to eat what fell from the rich man's table. Even the dogs came and licked his sores.
>
> The time came when the beggar died and the angels carried him to Abraham's side. The rich man also died and was buried.
>
> In hell, where he was in torment, he looked up and saw Abraham far away, with Lazarus by his side.
>
> So he called to him, 'Father Abraham, have pity on me and send Lazarus to dip the tip of his finger in water and cool my tongue, because I am in agony in this fire.'
>
> But Abraham replied, 'Son, remember that in your lifetime you received your good things, while Lazarus received bad things, but now he is comforted here and you are in agony.
>
> And besides all this, between us and you a great chasm has been fixed, so that those who want to go from here to you cannot, nor can anyone cross over from there to us.'
>
> He answered, 'Then I beg you, father, send Lazarus to my father's house,
> for I have five brothers. Let him warn them, so that they will not also come to this place of torment.'
>
> Abraham replied, 'They have Moses and the Prophets; let them listen to them.'
>
> 'No, father Abraham,' he said, 'but if someone from the dead goes to them, they will repent.'
>
> He said to him, 'If they do not listen to Moses and the Prophets, they will not be convinced even if someone rises from the dead.'
>
> (Luke 16: 19–31)

The reaction of Dives is that he wants to be able to warn his brothers about the need to care for the poor; but he is reminded that the prophets have been making this point for years.

In Matthew's Gospel, the parable of 'The Sheep and the Goats' shows how Jesus identified himself with the poor, so that caring for the poor is the same as caring for Jesus, and ignoring the poor is the same as taking no notice of Jesus:

IN YOUR NOTES

Look up the story in Mark 10: 17–22.

(a) What did the rich young man ask Jesus?

(b) What answer did Jesus give him?

FOR DISCUSSION

Do you think it is realistic for Christians today to give all their money to the poor?

Christians believe that caring for the poor is a very important part of their faith

When the Son of Man comes in his glory, and all the angels with him, he will sit on his throne in heavenly glory. All the nations will be gathered before him, and he will separate the people one from another as a shepherd separates the sheep from the goats.

He will put the sheep on his right and the goats on his left.

Then the King will say to those on his right, 'Come, you who are blessed by my Father; take your inheritance, the kingdom prepared for you since the creation of the world.

For I was hungry and you gave me something to eat, I was thirsty and you gave me something to drink, I was a stranger and you invited me in,

I needed clothes and you clothed me, I was sick and you looked after me, I was in prison and you came to visit me.'

Then the righteous will answer him, 'Lord, when did we see you hungry and feed you, or thirsty and give you something to drink?

When did we see you a stranger and invite you in, or needing clothes and clothe you?

When did we see you sick or in prison and go to visit you?'

The King will reply, 'I tell you the truth, whatever you did for one of the least of these brothers of mine, you did for me.'

Then he will say to those on his left, 'Depart from me, you who are cursed, into the eternal fire prepared for the devil and his angels.

For I was hungry and you gave me nothing to eat, I was thirsty and you gave me nothing to drink,

I was a stranger and you did not invite me in, I needed clothes and you did not clothe me, I was sick and in prison and you did not look after me.'

They also will answer, 'Lord, when did we see you hungry or thirsty or a stranger or needing clothes or sick or in prison, and did not help you?'

He will reply, 'I tell you the truth, whatever you did not do for one of the least of these, you did not do for me.'

Then they will go away to eternal punishment, but the righteous to eternal life.

(Matthew 25: 31–46)

Christians therefore believe that they have a duty to care for those in need. It is an expression of agape, reflecting the belief that every life is of value as being made 'in the image of God' (Genesis 1: 27).

IN YOUR NOTES

Make a summary of Biblical teaching about care for the poor, using some short quotations as examples.

CHRISTIAN BELIEFS IN ACTION

There are many different ways in which Christians might demonstrate a love and concern for the poor. For example:

- They might devote their lives to working with the poor in a developing country, as an aid worker in a refugee camp perhaps, or as a doctor or a nurse.
- If they cannot give their whole lives to work with the poor overseas, they might choose to do this for a short time, perhaps when they are students as a 'gap year', or perhaps with an organisation such as Voluntary Service Overseas (VSO) which organises placements for people who have special skills to offer.
- They could help in this country to support the work of those overseas. For example, they could work within the UK for a charitable organisation; they could spend a few hours each week helping in a charity shop, or they could take part in a street collection for an overseas aid agency, or they could make a door-to-door collection in their neighbourhood, perhaps during Christian Aid week. They might take part in fund-raising activities such as sponsored walks, marathon running or coffee mornings.
- A Christian could make an effort to live a simple lifestyle, buying only what is needed and resisting the temptation to have the most fashionable clothes or the most extravagant social life. The money saved could be given to charity.
- Christians might try not to be wasteful, by giving some thought to the amount of electricity they use, the amount of food they eat and so on. They could give discarded clothes and books to charity shops rather than throwing them away.
- Christians could take care when they are shopping to buy goods which carry a Fairtrade mark, and to avoid buying from companies which have a reputation for exploiting the poor. They could investigate the policies of the bank they use, and aim to deal as far as possible with businesses that show some concern for developing countries.

- Many Christians support the poor and the people who work with them through prayer.
- Christians could donate money to charity on a regular basis. Some do this by giving whatever they have spare, when they are asked. Others keep collection boxes for their chosen charity in their homes, and put money into it whenever they remember. Some Christians 'tithe', which involves giving up 10% of all income, to the poor and to the church. A popular way of giving is to set up a covenant, which involves paying a regular sum of money every month to charity. Charities can claim tax benefits on this form of giving, and it also helps them to work out a budget, because they can rely on a steady amount each month. Many Christians also include donations to charities in their wills.

FOR DISCUSSION

What do you think is a reasonable percentage of income for people in the Developed World to give to poorer countries?

Putting Christian beliefs into action

AID AGENCIES

Many people choose to work for charity or to give money to the poor, whether or not they are Christian. There are many different aid agencies which are not based on any religious beliefs, but which are motivated by the desire to do something about the injustice of world poverty. Organisations such as Oxfam, Save the Children Fund, Comic Relief and others do not have a basis in Christianity, but they do excellent work in an effort to help the world's poorest people.

In Christianity, helping the poor is not just a choice which some people might like to make if they are feeling particularly kind or they have a bit of spare money. It is the duty of Christians to care for the poor and the weak, it is something which they must do – an obligation.

> *What good is it, my brothers, if a man claims to have faith but has no deeds? Can such faith save him? Suppose a brother or a sister is without clothes and daily food. If one of you says to him, 'Go, I wish you well; keep warm and well fed,' but does nothing about his physical needs, what good is it? In the same way, faith by itself, if it is not accompanied by action, is dead.*
>
> (James 2: 14–16)

Because of this obligation, some aid agencies were started by Christians, and they work to try and put Christian beliefs into action.

TRAIDCRAFT

Traidcraft is a Christian organisation founded in 1979, with the aim of improving trade conditions for the developing countries, challenging the exploitation of the poor by the rich, and caring for the environment.

Traidcraft aims to:

expand and establish trading systems which are more just and which express the principles of love and justice fundamental to the Christian faith. Its objectives arise from a commitment to practical service and partnership for change, which puts people before profit.

Traidcraft imports and distributes handicrafts, fashion goods, stationery, tea, coffee, cocoa and foods produced by developing countries. It works in partnership with over 100 producers, to create opportunities for the poor by co-operating with them and enabling them to become more self-sufficient. The company advises the workers of goods which are likely to sell, and pays in advance for orders so that the poor are able to buy the raw materials without unnecessary hardship.

ICT FOR RESEARCH

Visit the Traidcraft web-site to have a look at the products for sale and to find out more about the people who produce them: www.traidcraft.co.uk

IN YOUR NOTES

Explain some of the main features of Fairtrade companies like Traidcraft. Show how the company tries to put its principles into action.

Traidcraft aims to help people become independent by producing goods which can be sold fairly

CHRISTIAN AID

HISTORY

Christian Aid is the official aid agency of over 40 different Church denominations in the UK and Ireland. It began just after the Second World War, as a response to the needs of many people in Europe who had lost their homes, families and all their possessions in the conflict. There were very many refugees who had absolutely nothing. The British and Irish churches set up an organisation called 'Christian Reconstruction in Europe', and raised a million pounds in donations, which was a huge sum of money for a time when so much had been destroyed and people had so little. Work began to help the refugees and to settle people back into a reasonable standard of living. In 1948, this work became part of the British Council of Churches.

During the 1950s and 1960s, as Europe began to settle down to peace-time, the focus began to move away from Europe to other countries where there was poverty and injustice, particularly Africa. The name changed to 'Christian Aid' to reflect the wider scope of the work that was being done, responding to poverty and disaster in many different countries:

Christian Aid
We believe in life before death

- In the 1970s, Christian Aid helped to give emergency relief to survivors of an earthquake in Peru; it responded to a drought in India, and to famine in Sudan and East Pakistan. By now Christian Aid was working in more than 40 different countries.

- In the 1980s, there was a major appeal for the victims of war in Lebanon. Doctors and nurses were flown out to give emergency help to the injured, and medicines and food were taken to the people. There was also a large development project in Ethiopia, taking emergency food and other supplies, and the construction of wells, education centres and hospitals.

- In the 1990s, Christian Aid was campaigning for fair trade and for an end to Third World debt. It was working to raise awareness of child labour and the child sex industry. Christian Aid also ran emergency appeals for Rwanda, the former Yugoslavia and Sierra Leone.

Today, Christian Aid works in more than 70 countries, on more than 700 local projects.

Aid workers try to help refugees who have nowhere to go because of war

Christian Aid is particularly keen to support women's projects

THE ROLE OF CHRISTIAN AID

Christian Aid is perhaps best known for giving emergency help to people who are the victims of disasters such as floods, earthquakes and famines. But although emergency relief does form a major part of Christian Aid's work, it is not the main role of the organisation. Christian Aid believes that it is important to take a long-term approach to poverty and injustice. Rather than waiting for a crisis to happen, Christian Aid works to make changes that will improve people's lives in a lasting way. It aims to give people skills and education, so that they can be self-reliant rather than having to depend on charity from other countries.

As well as providing food for emergencies, Christian Aid teaches people how to improve their farming methods so that they can become independent. It campaigns for fair wages to be paid to workers, and for fair trade conditions. Christian Aid provides medicines when there is disease, and it also becomes involved in health education and immunisation programmes, training local people to become nurses and midwives. It works to provide education, not only for children but also for adults

and especially for women, who rarely receive the same levels of education as men. Women are taught skills and crafts, so that they can produce goods which they can sell to support their families. Christian Aid is particularly supportive of women's projects, because often women are left to bring up their children unaided when their husbands are killed in wars or by terrorists.

CHRISTIAN AID FUND-RAISING

One of Christian Aid's most popular ways of raising money is by concentrating a lot of effort on to Christian Aid Week, in May each year. During this week there are television advertisements, poster campaigns, church collections, street collections and envelopes delivered door-to-door. People who may not be able to give up time to help Christian Aid on a regular basis throughout the year might feel they can take part in this special effort.

Christian Aid also raises money throughout the year in many other ways, including individual donations, money left by people in their wills, sales of goods such as Christmas cards, and local fund-raising activities such as sponsored walks.

CARITAS

Caritas is a world-wide Roman Catholic organisation which exists in more than 150 countries. This does not mean that it only offers help to Catholics; Caritas works for anyone who is in need, regardless of their race, nationality or religious beliefs. Caritas works among the powerless, the refugees, the marginal, the hungry, the exiles, and the homeless. Caritas Internationalis provides a network service between its different branches all over the world. It is a way of ensuring that accurate information is available and communicated between Catholic agencies in different countries, so that where there is a need, the response can be quick and appropriate.

Caritas believes that it is not enough to give people material help, such as food, clothing and medicines. It works in co-operation with poorer countries, to develop social projects which allow people to be self-reliant and to live in dignity. Its goals are explained as:

> fostering human promotion and providing the solidarity needed to nourish that hope which alone will enable our less fortunate brothers and sisters to take personal charge of their own lives and destiny and thus achieve that liberty which is their inalienable right as children of God.

The Catholic Church teaches that:

> If faith is not expressed in works, it is dead (cf. James 2: 14–16) and cannot bear fruit unto eternal life.
>
> (Catechism of the Catholic Church)

ICT FOR RESEARCH

Visit the Caritas Internationalis web-site to find out more about how Caritas operates in different parts of the world. See how the different needs in Kosovo, Rumania and Zambia, for example, are being tackled.

www.caritas.net

CAFOD

In England and Wales, Caritas is represented by CAFOD (Catholic Agency for Overseas Development). It is one of the United Kingdom's leading development and relief organisations, funding more than a thousand projects in Africa, Asia and the Pacific, Latin America, the Caribbean and Eastern Europe. It aims to get rid of poverty in the Developing World, and to bring about justice and fair shares for everyone.

CAFOD works in partnership with the local people in poor countries on over a thousand long-term projects, and also works within England and Wales in parishes, schools and community organisations, trying to help people to understand the causes of poverty.

At the heart of CAFOD is the Christian belief that everyone is made in the image of God, and that Christians should recognise Christ in each person. CAFOD states that its vision is for a world where:

- Everyone has a fair share of the good things of creation.
- The rights and dignity of each person are respected, discrimination is ended and people unite as a single human family from which no one is excluded.
- The voice of the poor is heard and lives are no longer dominated by greed.
- Everyone has access to food, shelter and clean water, to a livelihood, health and education.

HISTORY

CAFOD exists to put Christian beliefs into action. It began when the National Board of Catholic Women organised the first Family Fast Day in response to a request from the people of the Caribbean Island of Dominica for help with a mother and baby health care programme. Fasting continues to be one of CAFOD's methods of raising funds – people go without food, and give the money they would have spent to help the poor. Sometimes the fasts are sponsored. In this way, people are not only giving money, but are experiencing for a short while how it feels to be without food, and so their thoughts and prayers for the hungry have a greater focus.

In 1962, the Catholic Bishops of England and Wales officially set up CAFOD, the Catholic Fund for Overseas Development. They recognised that all sorts of local fund-raising projects were already going on, and they wanted to provide a central agency to organise all the efforts, and to keep people informed about different needs and the activities with which they could become involved.

By the time it was just ten years old, CAFOD was helping to fund 245 self-help projects in 40 countries. CAFOD, like Christian Aid, is strongly committed to self-help – rather than just handing out supplies to people in poverty, it believes in the importance of providing developing countries with the resources and skills that will help them to help themselves.

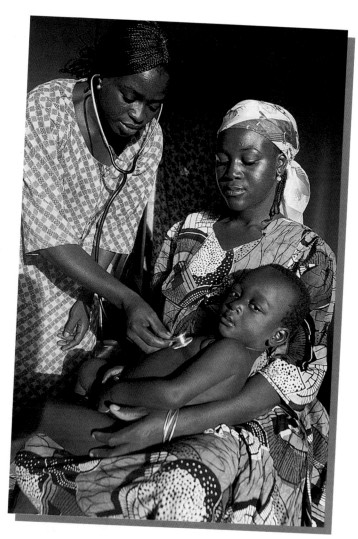

Healthcare is a major concern for CAFOD

ICT FOR RESEARCH

Visit the CAFOD web-site:

www.cafod.org.uk/

Find out more about CAFOD's work in emergencies; its campaigns for fair trade and for the cancellation of debt; its campaign against the use of landmines; its work with refugees. Find out more about the reasons why Christians might choose to support CAFOD.

TEARFUND

The Evangelical Alliance began in 1846, when a group of leaders from different evangelical churches formed a group, for support and to share ideas.

Tearfund began when, in 1968, a civil war in Nigeria left hundreds dead and many more suffering from the effects of famine. Christians sent money to the Evangelical Alliance to help the Nigerians, and a fund was set up, which became known as The Evangelical Relief Fund – or Tearfund. When it began, it had an income of £34,000. Today, it receives an annual income of over £20 million.

Tearfund is an evangelical Christian relief and development charity. 'Relief' means that it steps in, in times of emergency, to provide the basic equipment that people need in order to survive, such as food, medicines and blankets. 'Development' means that it is also concerned with longer-term projects. Like CAFOD and Christian Aid, it treats people in Developing countries as partners, and tries to work with them rather than for them, using local skills and expertise and responding to local needs. It believes that people should not have to be dependent on aid, but should be helped to achieve the skills and resources they need to be able to provide for themselves.

Tearfund believes that the poor, like the rich, are people, made in the image of God, and of equal value, regardless of their colour, religion or gender. It believes that the dignity of the poor should be respected.

There are many different projects in Developing Countries run by Tearfund. For example, Tearfund sent volunteers to refugee camps in Tanzania, Uganda, Burundi and Zaire to help provide food, shelter and medical care for the refugees fleeing from the war in Rwanda. In India and Africa, Tearfund workers provide medical care and support for people suffering from HIV and AIDS. In Haiti, education is being provided for children from poor families, who otherwise would not have the chance to go to school.

Tearfund also has a UK Action Fund, which helps churches in the UK to work with poor people in their own communities.

ICT FOR RESEARCH

Visit the Tearfund web-site:
www.tearfund.org
Find out more about the work of Tearfund. Look at some of the projects that are going on today, to use as examples in your writing. Find out how Tearfund tries to put Christian beliefs into action.

Christians believe that all human beings are made 'in the image of God', and deserve fair shares

PRACTICE EXAMINATION QUESTIONS

1 (a) Describe the work of a Christian organisation which helps the poor in developing countries. (8 marks)

Remember to choose an organisation that is specifically Christian. This question asks you to describe its work, so you should concentrate on giving examples of the different things it does, and not spend too much time on other aspects such as its history.

(b) Explain how Christians might show concern for the poor in their daily lives. (7 marks)

This question is about how Christians might put their faith into action in ordinary life, so you need to think about different ways they could do this. Try to mention several different ideas. Prayer is often a good idea to use in part (b) answers.

(c) 'It is not our responsibility if people in other countries are starving.' Do you agree? Give reasons to support your answer, and show that you have thought about different points of view. You must refer to Christianity in your answer. (5 marks)

Remember that for full marks you need to think about what a Christian might say, and give your own view, with reasons. If your views are the same as Christian views, you need to think of an alternative opinion as well to 'show that you have thought about different points of view.'

2 (a) Describe Christian teaching about care for the poor. (8 marks)

There are a lot of different ideas you could use here – the Bible, and teachings from the Churches and other Christian organisations. For example, statements by the Pope or by Christian Aid would also count as 'Christian teaching'. If you are referring to the Bible, you can mention parables such as 'The Sheep and the Goats' without having to tell the whole story in detail.

(b) Explain how a Christian might support the work of an organisation which deals with problems of world hunger. (7 marks)

Notice that this time, you are asked how a Christian might support an aid organisation. So you need not go into great detail about the organisation itself, but should concentrate on ways in which a Christian might support it, such as working in a charity shop or collecting door-to-door or fasting.

(c) 'Christians should give away all their money to the poor.' Do you agree? Give reasons to support your answer, and show that you have thought about different points of view. (5 marks)

Remember to support each point of view with reasons. In this answer, you might be able to think of Biblical reasons why a Christian might agree with the statement.

RELIGION, THE MEDIA AND ENTERTAINMENT

Today, people who live in developed societies have a wide range of media available to them. There are televisions, radios, newspapers, the Internet, cinemas, videos and DVDs, CD-ROMs, posters and advertisements; every day, people are surrounded by the media in its various different forms. It is the main source of information about what is going on in the world, and a favourite form of entertainment.

As well as providing information and entertainment, the media is a way in which people can share their beliefs and opinions, and try to influence the views of others. The important place that the media has in modern life can have **advantages** for Christians:

- Television and radio can be a good way for Christians to share their faith with a large number of other people. Christians can express their beliefs on television or on the radio, in the newspapers or via the Internet.

The media plays an important part in modern life

- Religious broadcasts provide a way for people to worship, even if they cannot get to church. People who are elderly, or sick, or who have small babies or live in remote parts of the country, can watch or listen to an act of worship from their own homes.
- Plays and films showing stories from the Bible or of the lives of famous Christians can bring these stories to life, so that they can be enjoyed by children or people who do not read very well or very often.
- The media can be a useful source of education. For example, many people learn about the problems of the environment, and what they can do to help, from television and newspapers. Newspapers and broadcasts show people what is going on in the world; they are a way of showing people the effects of famine, or earthquakes, or floods, and sometimes people are so interested in what they see that they are encouraged to go and do something about it. People have donated large sums of money to the victims of famine, and have taken help to countries such as Rumania, because of the things they have seen in the newspapers and on television. Christians believe that it is important to be aware of what is going on in the world, so that they can pray about it and try to help when people are in need.
- Religious and moral issues are often discussed on the television, on the Internet and in the newspapers. Christians can use these as opportunities to explain how their beliefs influence their moral decisions. They can defend Christian points of view in public through the media. Some Christians also feel that when television dramas raise important issues, such as abortion or homelessness, it provides a good opportunity for them to discuss the issue at home with the rest of their family.
- Aid organisations, charities and pressure groups, such as Christian Aid, Amnesty International or Tearfund, can use the media to advertise their activities and encourage other people to get involved. They use web-sites, television and newspaper advertisements to make more people aware of their work. Some organisations, such as The Samaritans, even do some of their work using the Internet – people can e-mail their problems and receive support in this way.

Some Christians, however, believe that the media has too much influence on modern life, and that it has some serious **disadvantages**:

- Watching television or using the Internet can be isolating. People spend a lot of their leisure time watching television, and they could have been using this time to talk to each other. In the evenings, many families sit in front of the television without saying a word to each other, even when they are eating.
- The media presents a view of the world that often does not fit with Christian teaching. In many television drama series, for example, the main characters are married and divorced several times, have affairs and commit crimes. The stories are interesting and entertaining, but they can give the impression that this sort of behaviour is normal and acceptable, and viewers might copy it.
- Some Christians believe that the media encourages people to be violent, when films are shown which seem to use violence as part of the entertainment. Many Christians feel uncomfortable about the way that violence is used to entertain people.
- Many Christians believe that pornography is wrong, because it can give the impression that women exist to be used by men, and it ignores the right purposes of sex. People who are in control of the media often make a great deal of money through the production and sale of pornography, particularly over the Internet.
- Although the media can be a way in which Christians share their beliefs and opinions, it can also be used by people who strongly disagree with Christianity. These people, too, can express their opinions and reach a wide audience. Some programmes make fun of Christianity and of Church leaders, in a way that believers might find offensive.
- Advertising can encourage people to be greedy and to consume more than they really need. It can emphasise the differences between rich and poor and make people feel inadequate or resentful. Many Christians believe that advertising promotes the wrong kind of values.

Some people believe that television prevents families from talking to each other

FOR DISCUSSION

Do you think it is right for Christian parents to try to control what their children watch on television?

FOR DISCUSSION

If Christianity was beginning today, rather than 2000 years ago, what methods do you think the first believers would use to publicise their message?

- The people who own the media are in the business of selling their products, and sometimes this can mean that sales become more important than other considerations, such as people's privacy or feelings. Christians might feel that the media often ignores the hurt that can be caused when stories are published about the private lives of famous people.

Some Christians believe that the media has such a bad effect on family life and on Christian values that they refuse to own televisions or to buy newspapers. Most Christians do read newspapers and watch television, and many use the Internet, but they often believe that they need to choose carefully what to read or watch. Christian parents are likely to try and make sure that their children only watch programmes or read magazines that are suitable for their age group and do not promote the wrong values. They are also likely to want to supervise their children when they use the Internet, especially if the children are quite young.

Christians have always tried to express their religious beliefs through whatever media were available to them. The Gospel stories were written down, copied by hand and circulated amongst the earliest Christians, and Christian thinking was publicised by letters. Today, there are very many more methods available to use in expressing beliefs and sharing them with other people.

EXPRESSING CHRISTIAN BELIEFS IN ART

Art is one form of media which has been in existence for almost all of the history of humanity. In some religions, it is believed that using art to illustrate God or important religious figures is very wrong. In Christianity, however, many people have found it helpful to use pictures, stained glass, sculptures and textile art to try and show what God is like or to bring religious stories to life. Christians often use different art forms when they decorate churches, so that people can learn about Christianity by looking around them as well as by listening to the service. Although some Christians, such as Baptists and the Society of Friends (Quakers), prefer simple surroundings in which to concentrate their minds on God, many others have found that representations of Bible stories in art help them to worship.

Some Christian denominations use art a great deal, to help worshippers think about aspects of God's nature

Christians have always used art as a way of expressing their beliefs

Some of the greatest paintings in history have come from the Christian tradition. Looking at the ways in which different artists imagine Jesus, or understand a Bible story, can often give the viewer a new and different understanding of the meanings of the story.

RELIGIOUS BROADCASTS

Christians often use television and radio as a way of sharing their beliefs. Special religious programmes are often called the 'God slot'; a time set aside in the schedule for the day or the week for religious broadcasts. Many Christians enjoy these, but some people think that religion should not be separated out from other kinds of programmes in this way, because it could give the impression that religion is a topic on its own that does not have much to do with ordinary life. Some Christians would like to see religious ideas more closely woven into all sorts of programmes, rather than kept apart.

TELEVISION EVANGELISM

'Television evangelism' is popular with some Christians, especially in America. Programmes are produced for cable or satellite television in which a preacher explains his or her understanding of the Christian message. There is often singing and prayers, and sometimes requests for the viewers to support the work of the programme with gifts of money.

Some Christians believe that television evangelism is a good way of making sure that as many people as possible hear about Christianity. Others think that it can sometimes be damaging, because the preachers might express views which are not shared by all Christians, or they might put too much emphasis on asking for money, and they might not always use the money they receive in ways that all Christians would support.

ICT FOR RESEARCH

Visit the web-site of the BBC:
www.bbc.co.uk/
Go to the 'what's on' page, and select 'Religion and Beliefs'. How many religious programmes are on BBC television and radio this week? Apart from religious worship, what other sorts of religious programmes are there?

ACTS OF WORSHIP

During the week, there are programmes on the radio and on the television which are called 'acts of worship'. They are broadcasts, often live, of people taking part in religious services. The viewer or listener can hear the sermon, and join in with the prayers and the hymns, even if they are unable to get to church. Many Christians enjoy 'Songs of Praise' on a Sunday, or listening to the daily service on Radio 4. The live broadcast of carols from King's College, Cambridge, is part of a traditional Christmas for hundreds of Christians. These programmes might encourage a Christian to think more about his or her faith when at home. They might make Christians more aware of being part of a wide community, sharing their faith with other people in different parts of the country, and people might enjoy seeing other Christians worshipping together on television, or hearing them on the radio.

However, some people also feel that perhaps it is not a good idea to have acts of worship as religious broadcasts, because it could make people less interested in going to church. People who have listened to a religious broadcast might feel that they do not need to go to church as well, and so they might miss the opportunity to meet with other Christians. Joining together with other worshippers has always been an important part of the Christian faith, and perhaps religious broadcasts discourage this.

LOOK UP

Look in the television section of the newspaper, or in the Radio Times or TV Times, and find out more about the religious programmes that are on this week. Are other religions represented, as well as Christianity?

Televised acts of worship can be enjoyed by people who are unable to get to church

DISCUSSION PROGRAMMES

Some programmes which involve Christianity take the form of discussions, where a moral or social issue is raised for a panel of people to discuss. This might be something like euthanasia, or genetic engineering, or attitudes towards foreign policy. Often, one or more of the people on the panel is a Christian, who tries to put forward a Christian point of view in response to the issue, and debates it with the other members of the panel. Most Christians support this kind of programme, because they see it as a good opportunity for a Christian point of view to be expressed, and it can show that Christianity has something relevant to say about modern issues.

ADVERTISING

Advertising is an important feature of society in developed countries. There are advertisements on the television and at cinemas, in newspapers and magazines, on the sides of buses, at sports events, on the Internet and in many other places; it is almost impossible for a day to go by in which we are not confronted by advertising.

Sometimes advertising can be a good thing. It can make us aware of new products that could make our lives easier, or draw our attention to ways in which we could save money. Many aid organisations spend a significant part of their income on advertising, to make people more aware of the work that they do and the problems they are trying to solve. Christian churches often use advertising themselves; they might put a colourful poster outside the church to advertise the events happening during the next month, or the Christian organisations that passers-by might like to join. Some churches advertise by producing newsletters about their activities and delivering them to nearby houses.

Often, advertising can be harmful. It can encourage people to think that they should spend more than they can really afford, because advertisements can give the impression that, without the product they are trying to sell, you will be less

successful, less attractive and lonelier. Advertisements try to make people feel discontented with what they already have. They suggest that there is something wrong with having grey hair, or a second-hand car, or clothes that you wore last year. They try to make us believe that other people are all leading more glamorous lifestyles than we are. Advertisements suggest that we have the right to treat ourselves to luxuries whenever we want them. We are encouraged to spend more and more on ourselves, even though three-quarters of the world have far less than we do.

Parents who are living on low incomes often find that advertising causes problems, because their children are encouraged to want things that the parents cannot afford. Especially in the weeks before Christmas, children are shown advertisements for expensive gifts, and they are given the impression that everyone else will be receiving presents of a similar value. This can lead the parents to get into debt.

Advertising can also cause problems by reinforcing prejudices and encouraging discrimination. When advertisers want to show a happy family enjoying food or a game together, they nearly always show a white family, suggesting that 'normal' families are white. Advertising often uses sexual stereotyping, giving the impression that women are interested in housework while men do outdoor jobs at home; it is rare to see an advertisement where a man gets excited about a dishwashing product or a woman enthuses about a tin of creosote.

FILMS ABOUT CHRISTIANITY

Some Christians believe that it is wrong to attempt to make films about the life of Jesus, because they say that he was such an important and special person that it would be wrong for an ordinary actor to pretend to be Jesus, or for someone to try and draw him or make a puppet of him for an animation. Sometimes, in order to make the story of the film fit together, the writers might decide to add a bit or to leave a bit out, and some Christians say that this is wrong because it takes something away from the truth of the Bible. Some films have been made which are based on the story of Jesus, but do not stick to it very closely. Others have used Bible stories as the basis for comedies, or for suggesting that aspects of Christianity are wrong; this is offensive to some Christians.

Other people believe that films, using actors or animation, can be a good way of presenting the messages of Christianity. Stories can be brought to life, and the films help the audience to imagine what it must have been like to have seen Jesus perform a miracle or to have heard him teach. Often, when Christians read the Bible or hear it being read, they concentrate on just a small part, maybe one parable or one incident, but a film can put the whole lot together and tell the Gospel story from beginning to end, which can have a far greater impact.

People might not enjoy reading books very much, but they might like to see films, and find them easier to understand. Films could be a good way of encouraging people to pay attention to Christianity and think about what it has to say.

CONCLUSION

Christians are not opposed to the media – the media is only a range of methods of communication, and Christians use them too. However, sometimes Christians are worried about some of the messages that are given through the media. The media has a great influence on the ways in which we understand the world, and it helps to shape our opinions. Most Christians, as well as many non-Christians, believe that people ought to realise that not everything in the media is good, and it should not all be believed as the truth.

'The Miracle Maker' is a film of the life of Jesus, presented in animation

INDEX